State Social Work
and the Working Class

Critical Texts in Social Work and the
Welfare State

General Editor: Peter Leonard

State Social Work
and the Working Class

Chris Jones

First published 1983 by
THE MACMILLAN PRESS LTD
London and Basingstoke
Companies and representatives throughout the world

ISBN 0 333 27160 2 (hard cover)
ISBN 0 333 27161 0 (paper cover)

Typeset in Great Britain by
STYLESET LIMITED · Salisbury · Wiltshire

Printed in Hong Kong

Contents

Acknowledgements

Over the three years of working on this book I have benefited
from the encouragement and help of many friends, and I thank
them warmly for their support. My greatest debt, however,
is to Tony Novak, without whose help and comradeship this
book would never have been completed. He has read through
countless drafts, corrected my grammar, cooked dinners and
been my sternest critic and my greatest support. Finally, I
would like to thank the editor of the series Peter Leonard
and my publisher Steven Kennedy, both of whom have
patiently offered wise comment and encouragement.

Rochdale, England   CHRIS JONES
October 1982

List of Abbreviations

BASW	British Association of Social Workers
CCETSW	Central Council for Education and Training in Social Work
COS	Charity Organisation Society
CQSW	Certificate of Qualification in Social Work
CSS	Certificate of Social Service
CTSW	Council for Training in Social Work
MSC	Manpower Services Commission
NALGO	National Association of Local Government Officers
NAPO	National Association of Probation Officers
NUPE	National Union of Public Employees
SWT	*Social Work Today*

Editor's Introduction

The relationship between welfare 'clients', social workers and the local authority which employs them has long been considered a problematic triangular one. During the 1950s and 1960s, when psychoanalytic-based therapy seemed to be the goal of many aspiring social workers, or at least of *writers* about social work, almost all attention was focused on the social worker–client relationship – on emotional exchanges, on identification, on dependence, on 'problems with authority' and on transference and counter-transference within the relationship. Totally absent at this time was any serious attention, beyond a fascination with 'sub-cultural differences', to the essentially class nature of the relationship. Later, from the early 1970s, as social services organisations grew in size and complexity and as the managerial component expanded and became more confident, social workers experienced mounting problems in their organisational roles. At the same time, increasing emphasis was given to the monitoring and control of individuals and families considered deviant or 'at risk', culminating in various moral panics, most notably in the area of 'non-accidental injury' to children.

The specific experiences of this triangular relationship by welfare clients, social workers and social services managers and local councillors, may be considered as a microcosm of a broader structural relationship: that between the working class, the occupation of social work, and the state apparatus. To consider the relationship in these latter terms is to transform immediately our understanding of it, for it provides the possibility of contextualising specific experiences in terms of their historical development and their current political and ideological significance.

But once we step back from the immediate experiences of this relationship and attempt to understand their context, we find that many interpretations of it exist. Most significant, for our purposes, are on the one hand those who see the relationship as essentially *benign*, and on the other hand those who find it wholly *malignant* and *oppressive*.

There can be little doubt, of course, that the dominant view of the relationship between the state, social work and the working class is that it is essentially designed to be *caring*, and even where such care includes control, it operates, though they often fail to realise it, in the interests of the working class as well as of the state. This benign vision is the cornerstone of the social-democratic reformist conception of the welfare state and underpinned all the efforts during the 1970s to 'reform the welfare' from the Seebohm Committee onwards. It was a conception of the relation between the welfare state and the working class which was especially significant to David Donnison's failed attempt, whilst Chairman of the Supplementary Benefits Commission, to use a part of the state apparatus in the interests of the poor.

More recently, it is the ideology of the Barclay Report and most especially in its proposals for 'community social work'. A basic notion in the Report is that there must be a *partnership* between working-class communities and local authority social services, and it is argued that despite failure in the past this partnership is still possible. As an exercise in the attempted mystification of class relations, the Barclay Report makes interesting reading. It is unlikely, however, to impress working-class communities who experience their relationship with social workers and the local welfare apparatus predominantly as control, subordination and incorporation, a relationship more likely to be characterised by antagonism than by partnership. In the 1970s and early 1980s, the social-democratic welfare consensus has come under challenge from two distinct quarters. So far as the radical Right is concerned, it sees the relationship between the state, social work and the working class as *too benign*, and in some respects takes a more realistic view of the strict limits to which welfare reform can be pushed without revealing basic antagonisms.

Given the failure of welfare reformism in recent years to improve the position of the working class, it is not surprising that social-democratic prescriptions have also come under increasing challenge from a left critique which sees the relationship between the state, social workers and the working class as essentially based on oppression and control. Such an approach has the special virtue of unmasking the hypocrisy of much current discussion in the social work and social policy fields, and of revealing its underlying function, the justification of the present structure of class, gender and ethnic relations. But as the economic and social crisis deepens and is paid for by the increased oppression and suffering of the working class, it becomes increasingly urgent for the Left to develop this analysis into a coherent picture of the interaction between state welfare and the working class.

It is this task to which Chris Jones applies himself in his new book. Continuing the work of previous volumes in this series, *State Social Work and the Working Class* builds, through detailed empirical evidence and historical analysis, an impressive picture of the interaction between welfare clients and social workers within the state apparatus. The story which Chris Jones has to tell could in no way be characterised as primarily one of benign results for the working class, or even less of benign intentions on behalf of the state apparatus. On the other hand, Chris Jones's account shows how ambiguous and problematic for the state is the use of social workers as instruments of intervention and control in the lives of the working class. Although he differs in some important respects from two previous volumes in the series concerned specifically with social work, namely Corrigan and Leonard's *Social Work Practice Under Capitalism*, and Bolger, Corrigan, Docking and Frost's *Towards Socialist Welfare Work*, Chris Jones is essentially pursuing the same project — the careful analysis of the contradictions involved in the triangular relationship.

The contradiction central to Chris Jones's analysis is that involved in training, using and controlling a social stratum or class fraction — state employees — for the purposes of managing the working-class poor. He shows us how continuously unreliable social workers have been in this role, and describes to what lengths the state welfare apparatus and its training organisations have gone in attempting to ensure their loyalty. But social workers have continued to be *contaminated* by this contact with the working-class poor — a material experience deeply challenging to dominant ideologies. Although, as Chris Jones demonstrates, the state has been in a large measure successful in fragmenting the poor from the rest of the working class, even this strategy continues to be problematic, especially as the crisis deepens and, especially through unemployment, affects the working class as a whole.

For social workers, and others, experiencing the full impact of the control exercised over them and their work from within the state welfare apparatus, this book is most important. In particular, it shows us that to understand this control, including the subordination of social workers' judgements to the interests of welfare management, we must go beyond thinking only in terms of the effects of bureaucratic organisation, careerism and the failure of nerve in the face of moral panics, significant as these are. We must see the relationship between the state, social workers and the working class as one response to specific problems facing an advanced capitalist country in decline, namely how to control the working class and especially its poorest elements and so ensure that the balance of class forces remains safely in the interests of capital.

Chris Jones's stimulating book demonstrates again that the view of the welfare relationship as wholly oppressive is a too simple one. The contradictions and strains in that relationship provides, even in these dark days, the opportunity for social workers, these 'difficult employees', to aim for a different, more socialist, relationship with the working class.

University of Warwick   PETER LEONARD
October 1982

1

Introduction: Restructuring Social Work

That state social work has recently entered a new phase in its development is beyond question. This new phase has been signalled by many changes and indicators, some large and others small, but all significant in their cumulative effect. One of the clearest indications of this shift in direction has been in the rapid and acute reductions in personal social services expenditure, with annual growth rates of over 10 per cent per annum between 1969 and 1974 plummeting to cuts of around 1—3 per cent since. The impact of these reductions has been magnified by the consequences of the recession. Levels of unemployment unparalleled in Britain's post-war period have combined with inflation and all-round reductions in the social wage provided by state welfare to both deepen and widen the extent of acute poverty. Thus a report published by the Association of Directors of Social Services on the implications of the cuts states that 'never has poverty in material terms been such a major factor in whether people (particularly children) require to be "in care", or can survive in the community' (cited in *CHC News*, December 1981). When the consequences of the dramatic increase in the proportion of elderly people within the population are added to this picture it is quite evident that the personal social services are faced with impossible demands and pressures at the very time when their budgets are being reduced.

Situated as they are within local authorities there has been some variation to the response of social services departments in the face of these pressures and changed circumstances.

Nevertheless, notwithstanding some important local variations, it is possible to identify some broad lines of development which characterise a general shift in the character of state social work. Significant among these has been a general reduction in the service provision of local authority social services departments. Since approximately 1976 there have been successive cutbacks in the provision of home helps (often accompanied by increased charges), meals on wheels, aids and adaptations for the handicapped, day-care facilities, holiday assistance for carers and their dependants, telephones for the housebound, luncheon clubs and discretionary financial assistance. The social services budget of the City of Manchester for 1982—3 typifies this process of weakening service provision, with £65,000 being 'saved' in the provision of aids and adaptations and transport for handicapped persons, a 10 per cent reduction in the meals-on-wheels service coupled with a 5p increase in the charges for a meal leading to a £95,000 'saving'; £128,000 is recouped by increasing charges for day nursery places and reducing the staff in each nursery by one.

The Manchester budget also indicates the manner in which residential provision has been a target of successive cutbacks. In 1982—3 this authority proposes to close one old persons' home and two family group homes as well as providing fewer wardens for those in sheltered accommodation. These cuts are merely the latest casualities, and most local authorities have been compelled to reduce their service provision annually since 1976. These reductions do not, however, reflect a decreasing demand by clients for these services.

Even prior to these reductions the demand for services often outstripped their availability. This entailed social workers in considerable assessment work in order to ration and distribute available resources to those deemed to be in the greatest need. The subsequent cuts, however, have been of such a scale that new rationing strategies have had to be implemented and devised, with priority groups of clients being more precisely defined. Many clients have suffered in this process, either experiencing a blanket refusal for a service that could have brought valuable relief, or the indignity of more penetrative investigation to ensure their eligibility for assistance.

For many social workers these latest developments have been disturbing. A large number of those now employed in local authority social services departments came into social work as a result of the rapid expansion in state social work following the 1968 Seebohm Report and subsequent re-organisation. For a decade until the cuts in public welfare spending took effect, social work had experienced a period of rapid growth as successive governments increasingly came to regard it as a discrete welfare agency in its own right with a potential for 'treating' such persistent social problems as juvenile delinquency and 'problem family' poverty and nuisance. Training courses expanded, thousands of new posts were created and the statutory duties of social work extended. For social work the late 1960s seemed like the realisation of a long and cherished dream. The formation of social services departments, coupled with such significant legislation as the 1969 Children and Young Persons Act were widely acknowledged as marking a new dawn for social work. Freed from its previous subordination to the medical profession and with official sanction for its individualised treatment philosophy, it seemed as though the long struggle through the 1950s and early 1960s to gain recognition and a slice of the welfare state of its own had been successful. It is against this climate of optimism for the future that the implications of the recent measures of constraint and change have to be weighed.

Even before the first round of major cuts in 1976 it was evident that the reality of social work did not match up to the dream of the future which was envisaged in 1968. Within the mainstream of the profession there was little evidence of preparedness for the consequences of reorganisation. For many the new social services departments were not experienced as the new fertile ground for social work practice, at least of the variety taught on many professional courses. Rather, they were complex and unresponsive bureaucratic organisations with long and hierarchical command structures which involved social workers in time-consuming bureaucratic servicing work (form-filling) and a substantial diminution in their ability to control and direct their work with clients. Similarly, it was also becoming apparent well before 1976 that the reorganisation of social work had in practice resulted in reinforcing social work's subordinate relationship to the existing primary welfare state agencies such as the housing, social security, health and education authorities.

Thus as the distinctive treatment elements of social work continued to be under-resourced or neglected, typified by the partial implementation of the 1969 Children and Young Persons Act and the qualified support to the 1970 Chronically Sick and Disabled Persons Act, the rationing, constraining and controlling elements of social work were given new emphasis and importance. For, quite contrary to the Seebohm Committee's assertion that the reorganised social services would make social work more accessible to clients and potential clients and thereby better able to meet need, the reality has been in improving the access of other statutory and official bodies which have increasingly turned to social work as being a means of unloading some of their more difficult consumers and customers. According to the 1982 Barclay Report on social work, over 60 per cent of the client referrals to social services departments come from official third parties, including housing and education departments, social security and health authorities, police and the courts, and more recently the public utility boards of water, gas and electricity.

This pattern of referral and the manner in which other state agencies have turned to social work has had an accelerating effect over the past decade in changing the emphasis and character of state social work. Unlike clients, these referral agents have considerable power to define the problem and the solution which they expect the social services department to achieve. With respect to fuel boards, for example, they have defined the majority of their referrals as debtors, and the solution and task of the social worker is defined as ensuring an ability to pay backed up with the threat of disconnection for failure or refusal to co-operate. Many of the referrals made by third party statutory and official agencies conform to this pattern and have pushed social work towards being the servicing and dustbin agency of the welfare state in which the discretion and autonomy of social workers and their ability to undertake the in-depth relationship work with clients which is at the heart of the activity have been significantly reduced and modified. Moreover, this trend has rapidly accelerated as the twin forces of cuts and recession have taken their toll within these primary state agencies. Thus, as social security benefits have been reduced and large areas of discretion removed following the two 1980 Social Security Acts (Novak, 1981), and as fuel and rent bills have increased along with poverty and social stress, so statutory agencies have turned with increasing regularity to the local authority social services in order to relieve their burden and problems.

Albeit for often very different reasons, these changes in social work and the welfare state generally have been profoundly depressing and damaging for clients and social workers alike. For many clients this restructuring of the welfare state has resulted in a marked diminution of services and resources, many of which had a crucial role in their survival. Furthermore, many clients now confront a distinctly more hostile 'welfare' state, more reluctant to consider their problems sympathetically and more stringent and conditional in the aid it offers. Likewise, many of those social workers who deal directly with clients are only too well aware of the manner in which the state has 'toughened up' over recent years and the manner in which the liberal ideas of client welfare are rapidly losing their meaning in contemporary social services departments. After all, despite the various interpretations that can be placed on 'client welfare', it would not seem naive to suggest that a great majority of those employed as social workers entered this occupation because of some commitment to the 'betterment' of the dependent and residual poor and so for whom rationing and withdrawing assistance, and being compelled to assist the state to undermine the already precarious existence of clients, are contrary to their beliefs.

For many social workers this latest phase in the development of state welfare and social work has provoked many responses, anxieties and questions. Those who have not been victims of resigned defeat or not decided to keep their heads down in order to secure their career prospects in a climate where 'troublemakers' have been disciplined and even black-listed (Lang and Castledine, 1979) are trying to develop strategies appropriate to the new situation. The development and extension of trade unionism among social workers is profoundly significant in this respect and is opening up new possibilities for social workers who are intent upon both defending social work clients from further attacks and trans-forming the nature of welfare generally. However, the pressure on these progressive social workers is considerable. The management of appearances has now become a major occupa-tional concern for many radical and critical social workers employed in increasingly authoritarian departments. The constant turning down of requests for help and assistance by clients is emotionally exhausting and the stuff of nightmares. There has also been a marked increase in criticism of social work by conservative opinion which has long rejected the more liberal and humanitarian ethos of social work and has seized with enthusiasm the shift to the right to press home its attacks. These attacks have become more significant in that they have been endorsed by influential state agencies and personnel, including the police and judiciary, who would like to see the powers of social work greatly reduced particularly in the area of juvenile delinquency and non-accidental injury.

Unfortunately for progressive social workers these criticims have not engendered any significant public response from clients or working-class organisations. While there have been a few exceptions, for example during the 1978–9 strike social workers in Liverpool were supported by the local trades council and car workers at the Ford plant, there has been no general national defence of social work by organised labour in the face of cuts and restructuring. There are a number of reasons for this, including the strained relationship between significant clusters of the client population and organised labour, coupled with a long tradition of suspicion towards social work as a predominantly middle-class moralistic welfare activity which hinders rather than assists solutions to working-class problems of poverty. While there has been (and still is) some justification for these perceptions of social work, the distancing of organised labour from this now important part of the state's welfare system has denied support for those many liberals and radicals currently employed as welfare workers. This lack of support has discouraged and disheartened many progressive social workers — and has contributed to the growth of apathy and cynicism among others — who rightly believe that state social work does contain within it some valuable gains for clients which could be extended and secured if only popular pressure could be applied. Furthermore, in the broader political perspective the practice of social work reveals many important insights into the nature of contemporary capitalist society and the state and identifies with particular clarity the limits of welfare. For these insights to be influential in the construction of a socialist alternative a more fruitful and positive relationship between progressive social workers and organised labour needs to be developed.

These themes and issues constitute some of the major preoccupations of this book. The tasks confronting social workers have never been easy, and in recent years the pressures have increased significantly. For those social workers who see their work for the state as being an important area of struggle and refuse to allocate their political work to 'after-hours' activism the recent and current restructuring of the welfare state with its central thrust of re-ordering the relationship between working people and the state has yielded a surfeit of issues and campaigns. The consequences of repressive social security policies, racist nationality laws, the appalling increase in poverty and despair, the manner in which community-care policies are reinforcing the subordination of women and subjecting them and the dependants for whom they care to new depths of misery, the accelerating drift to more punitive policies with respect to young offenders, are just some of the issues currently facing social workers and demanding attention.

Thus the problems for many social workers today are not ones of identifying the issues which require attention but rather of determining the most appropriate sites where energies can be used most effectively and of devising strategies which both widen the campaigns and reconcile short-term objectives with the longer-term struggle to change society radically. It is this cluster of problems which have decisively influenced the writing of this book and largely determined its structure and content. The resolution of some of these difficulties must start with a firm understanding of the nature and development of contemporary state social work. Through analysing this development and by drawing out the complex and contradictory forces which have shaped state social work and its dynamic relationship to the client population it is possible to identify more precisely the progressive features of social work and its political potential for contributing to the construction of a socialist alternative.

The book falls roughly into two halves. In Chapters 2 and 3 the focus is on the clients of social work, analysing the way in which the state has identified and attempted to deal with the problems they pose. Chapter 4 examines the relationship of clients to the non-client working class. The second half of the book focuses primarily on the social workers themselves and seeks to demonstrate the many difficulties and problems which have confronted the state in employing concerned and often liberal social workers and directing them to intervene deeply into the lives and circumstances of some of the most deprived and impoverished victims of contemporary society.

Emerging from this discussion and constituting a central theme of the book is that the development of social work has been immensely problematic and difficult for the state. This is due in no small part to the sensitive character of the domain of social work, the residual and dependent poor who constitute the bulk of social work's client population. This section of the population constantly threatens to be a political embarrassment given that they represent some of the principal human victims of a society structured upon the pursuit of profit. The pattern and pace of social work's development has been decisively influenced by the state's concern to present clients in a manner which does not challenge the legitimacy of capitalism and expose its evident disregard for those it regards as superfluous and its contempt for those it has denied the opportunities for securing their well-being. By recognising this key feature and through unravelling the way in which it has been fought over (and continues to be so) it is possible to identify with greater clarity the areas in which social workers can effectively direct their energies in the struggle for a just and humane society.

2

The Clients of Social Work

INTRODUCTION

New directions in social work will prove as under-productive as the old ones unless they are based on a clear understanding of [social workers'] ... role in society.

(Beaumont, 1976, p. 74)

Since its modern origins in the middle of the last century, social work has been one of the many strategies developed and deployed by the ruling class and the state for intervening in the lives of the working-poor. Although the motives of individual social workers have always been rich and varied, and many have been genuinely moved by and concerned with the consequences of poverty for sections of the population, as an 'institution' social work has to be considered as one of the agencies of class control and regulation in Britain. That is not to say that social work is a pure product of the ruling class or that it has not been affected significantly by working-class pressure, but rather to identify social work's prevailing intent in society.

For many social workers this class-control character of the activity saturates indirectly and directly virtually every aspect of their daily work; there is no escape from it. One of the sites where this character is most evident is in the relationships of social workers and the social services departments with their clients. That such relationships are class relationships is evident not only in that the majority of social workers are white middle class and the majority of clients are working class, but also in the actual content and style of the interventions. The very notions of social problems and pathology within this society are political constructs defined more often than not by the dictates of capitalist political economy rather than with respect to the human needs of clients (Davis, 1938; Mills, 1943). Thus while problems of poverty, delinquency, family breakdown, sickness and old age are problems for the working class, it is common to discover that when the state intervenes in these 'problems' the policies enacted often reflect and embody values and concerns different from those who are in difficulty.

Many social workers are only too well aware of this orientation in state social policy. They know full well, for example, that it is no real answer to a client's fuel poverty simply to introduce forms of budgeting that may delay or avoid a disconnection. Similarly, many are also aware that a young offender's attendance at an intermediate treatment group for twelve weeks is hardly going to change the circumstances which led to the youngster's offence, or the methods of policing which propel so many working-class youngsters before the courts.

One senses among many social workers a more guarded approach to the possibilities of social work as a means of improving the life-chances and conditions of many clients. Indeed, there is a substantial number of social workers employed in local authority social services departments who have now spent the majority of their 'professional' life under the constant threat and reality of expenditure cuts. For these and many other welfare workers the idealism which characterised the expansion of social work after 1945 is no longer appropriate or relevant. There are now many who would reject as naive and over-zealous the claims made by Sir Charles Morris in his address to the Institute of Almoners in 1964:

Tremendous things are beginning to be thought possible through the social services and it is coming to be recognised that the size and quality of its army of social workers is one of the things by which the health and prospects of a modern advanced community can most surely be judged . . . it is now coming to be agreed . . . that the health and

happiness of a society, and also its future, depend upon
the size and quality of its body of social workers.

(Morris, 1964, p. 56)

The purpose of this chapter is to start the process of building
up a more appropriate understanding of the nature of social
work. This is done by exploring the nature of the state's
interest in and relationship with clients. Why is it that some
people, or some sections of the population, become seen and
defined as clients? In this chapter some of the general characteristics of the client population are shown, before moving on
to consider some of the economic forces that have shaped
social work's development and the state's increased intervention in the lives of the poor. The following chapter broadens
the analysis by exploring the political issues and debates which
have affected the treatment of clients, as well as indicating
some of the more significant contradictions which have emerged
over the past thirty-five years.

WHO ARE THE CLIENTS?

If one were to ask the question 'Who are the clients of social
work?' of a group of social policy or social work students, it
is likely that a long list of 'conditions' would be the reply.
After all, most of the books on social work break down the
clientele in this way and talk of the mentally and physically
handicapped, the elderly, single-parent families, juvenile
delinquents and 'children in trouble', problem families, and
so on. Apart from allocating clients to one of these accepted
classifications there is rarely any attempt to draw out any
points of similarity between them. Indeed, it is assumed that
we all know and accept that the differences between an
elderly person and a child in trouble are so great that it would
be ridiculous to bother ourselves with comparisons and the
seeking out of common threads. Yet, just as there are obvious
empirical differences between clients there are also some fairly
obvious similarities. The most patent of these concerns their

class position and their related material circumstances. In the main, the clients of social work are working class and poor.

In one of the few (but now dated) studies of a (pre-Seebohm) social welfare department, Jeffrys discovered that social workers saw more clients who

> occupied caravans, lived at high densities, and had not the exclusive use of some domestic amenities than of those whose housing circumstances were more advantageous ... The households were headed by men [sic] from all social classes, but with the exception of some health service workers, were those of manual rather than non-manual middle class workers, and amongst the manual workers, of semi- and unskilled workers rather than of skilled men.
>
> (Jeffrys, 1965, p. 47)

Although there is much more to be said about the nature of poverty and its effects on people's lives than was ever re-counted in Jeffrys's study, there can be little doubt that it is poverty and its consequences which are crucial factors in why many people become clients of social services departments. Indeed, even Frederick Seebohm estimated in 1969, before the current depression, that poverty and bad housing 'prob-ably caused something like 60% of the work that is now carried on by social workers' (cited in Sinfield, 1970, p. 34).

Despite the fact that there has been some awareness within mainstream social work that the majority of their clients are drawn largely from specific sections of the working-class poor, this characteristic of the client population tends to be obfus-cated and underplayed. Instead, social work has attempted to deal with clients in ways which either deny or marginalise the class dimension through focusing on intermediate categories which define individuals in terms of some externally identified characteristic. However, labels such as 'problem family', 'delinquent', 'mentally or physically handicapped', etc., are very partial categories, and moreover are deeply conservative, for they virtually ignore the class context of poverty, inequality and powerlessness, which are crucial for understanding the nature of clients' problems and difficulties. In Chapter 4 some of the consequences of this depoliticising approach to clients are considered in detail.

Nevertheless, there are more crucial characteristics to being a social work client than being working class and poor. After all, working-class poverty has been a continuous feature of capitalist production, whereas state social work is a far more recent phenomenon. More conclusively, it is also apparent that only a minority of the working-class poor become clients and are deemed to require social work intervention. In the rest of this chapter, therefore, those particular features that distinguish clients and which have decisively influenced the state's development of social work are discussed. The client's relationship to the wage labour market can be identified as being of special significance.

CHILD CARE

A particularly crisp illustration of the importance of this labour dimension to the development of state social work is to be found in the formation of the child care service during the first decade after the Second World War. During these years there was an acute shortage of labour, and anxieties over the future supply of domestic labour were compounded by the dire predictions of demographic developments produced by Political and Economic Planning (1948) and the Royal Commission on Population (1949). Both of these reports warned of continual labour shortage due to the dip in the birth rate and longer-term social pressures due to the growing proportion of the very old in the population.

As some writers have noted (e.g. Wilson, 1977, 1980), these shifts in the labour market led many employers to turn increasingly to women and blacks to undertake the often menial and unpleasant jobs that could not be filled from the native male work-force. But as the PEP report warned, the demand for women in the wage labour force contradicted the corresponding demand for more children to swell the supply of labour, and most importantly put at some risk the future *quality* of labour as the socialisation of children would be impaired by the partial absence of women from the home:

> From the point of view of the community, the conflict between work and motherhood is particularly acute at the moment. Women are the nation's largest reserve of labour, and at present every additional pair of hands is badly needed. The government's manpower policy has emphasised the need for women to enter industry. But if both the quantity, and even more importantly, the quality of the future population are to be safeguarded, women must be given more time now to the bearing and rearing of children.
>
> (PEP, 1948, p. 170)

The anxiety about labour at this time was reflected across all areas of state social policy and was articulated in a wide variety of ways; one of the most notable was this debate about the role of women, especially married women with children, in the labour market. With respect to the development of the personal social services, it was this concern which was especially important in the development of the child care service in 1948, and in the renewed interest in problem families.

In the debates surrounding the development of the child care service, and the general extension of the state through social work, a common concern was expressed about the large number of children who were 'spoiled' for the labour market and good citizenship by their family background and upbringing (Home Office, 1951, pp. 44—5). Thus, as Martin (1944, p. 106) remarked at the time, given the pincer movement of a declining birth rate and an increasing elderly population, it was imperative that, 'quite apart from humanitarian considerations, every child should be given the maximum chance of survival, and more important still, should reach adult life in as perfect a state of physical and mental health as is practicable'.

The evacuation programme during the war, followed by the growing involvement of social work agencies such as the Family Service Units among the slum populations of inner cities (Titmuss, 1950; Stephens, 1945), heightened awareness about the ways in which a substantial cluster of the population seemed to be locked in poverty and destitution. Popularly known as the 'problem families', writer after writer (Timms & Philp, 1957) drew attention to the manner in which these families not only constituted a huge drain on the newly expanded range of state welfare resources, but also produced more than the average number of children, many of whom never made it to the labour market in an employable state. Instead, many of these children were apparently lost to production in that their early socialisation tended to encourage attitudes and values that were more likely to lead to a career in crime and delinquency rather than 'honest' wage labour. Consequently, at a time of acute labour shortage and the projected demographic trends produced by the Royal Commission on Population, it was hardly surprising that there should be renewed attention on this section of the working-class poor. As one MP stated during the debate on the Children Bill, 'From the national point of view we cannot afford to lose 12,000 children or have their lives wasted' (Lindsay, *Hansard*, 28 June 1948); or as the PEP Report noted, 'to cut down the wastage of human assets is to reduce the difficulties which confront a population policy' (1948, p. 137).

It was consequently no historical accident that the first major step taken in the post-war expansion of the personal social services was the formation of the child care service under the auspices of the Home Office in 1948. Given the shortages in labour supply and little prospect of any sustained improvement the government looked to the child care service as being one of the means whereby wasted and spoiled labour could be rescued and rehabilitated. This labour dimension also helps us to explain why state strategies directed at this cluster of the poor moved away during these years from punitive containment (symbolised by the Poor Law) towards a softer treatment and rehabilitative approach epitomised by the casework of the Children's Officers. Although this significant shift in the styles of intervention also involved political considerations (discussed in the next chapter), the scarcity of labour at a time of high demand compelled the state to adopt a rehabilitative approach in contrast to the neglect and containment strategies which had prevailed in the inter-war period when so much 'good' surplus labour was available.

The importance of this relationship between clients and the state of the labour market is further illuminated by the changes currently taking place in state social work as unemployment rises well over three million. With such a large pool of surplus labour there is no longer any pressing need to rescue potential labour from the working-class poor. As the compulsion for rehabilitation has been removed, so the focus has shifted towards containment and control. Services which at one time were seen as being necessary to the restorative work of schools and social workers — nurseries, play groups, remedial education — have all experienced a disproportionate reduction in resources and support. It would seem from Bernard Davies's work (1980, 1981) that the youth and community service provides clear evidence of this shift towards toughness and constraint in what was once seen to be a vital service for rehabilitating generally disaffected and alienated youth for the labour market and social conformity. Unfortunately for restorative agencies such as social work and the youth and community service there is very little evidence to suggest that their efforts in rehabilitative work during the past thirty years have been widely effective. Such an inability to indicate clear treatment results has undoubtedly weakened the authority of social work to resist the restructuring which is pushing it towards a more narrow and rationing role within state welfare, discussed in Chapter 1.

THE PROBLEM OF COST

While official anxieties in the late 1940s about a long-term shortage in labour created a climate favourable to renewed attention on the 'submerged tenth' who had been largely ignored and neglected by the inter-war governments, and offered the opening for a rehabilitative strategy based on social work, so too the renewed attention on 'problem families' brought to light another compelling factor which was to force the state to act — the problem of cost.

Mere material poverty, however desperate, does not explain why some people become clients. To become a client a person has to be in one way or another a *nuisance*. There are many forms this nuisance can take, but one which has been given increasing prominence is that of cost. Interestingly, as the microscope of official concern lowered on problem families after the Second World War, more and more writers drew attention to the costs which these families imposed on many state resources. Thus as early as 1953 social workers such as Howarth were focusing on the parasitical behaviour of problem families as being the most important characteristic of their social problem status:

> What is the real social problem? This might be assessed fairly well in terms of the cost to the community in social services such as children taken into care, children and adults appearing in the courts, the dilapidation of housing, etc. More intangible would be the lack of family training of future citizens.
>
> (Howarth, 1953, p. 767)

Similarly, in one of the books which did much to publicise the dangers of the problem families Tom Stephens placed great emphasis on this high-cost dimension:

> These are the problem families. [That] they are a reproach to the community and a disgrace to our social services needs no emphasis. One can go further. Their cost to the community in terms of social service is altogether disproportionate to their numbers. Almost the entire apparatus for the prevention of child neglect exists to combat the effects of this social disease, and the breaking up of the neglected home leaves a pathetic trail of children orphaned by the law, who must be cared for by institutional homes or private foster parents. To school attendance officers, health visitors, housing managers, relieving officers, and many others, they are a burden, each demanding as much attention as many normal families and deriving little benefit from the services they receive.

In terms of social disservice their cost may be even higher. Dr. Cyril Burt has shown the extent to which such sordid homes are responsible for mentally and educationally backward children. Their low standards are passed on from one generation to another, not so much through heredity, though often the least fit, mentally and physically are the most prolific, but mainly because their children are stunted by neglect and handicapped by atrocious up-bringing. J. H. Bagot in his study *Juvenile Delinquency* stressed that juvenile delinquency is most frequently caused by the combination of evil circumstances found in these homes, and remarks that 'juvenile delinquency is concentrated in one section of the population, the very poor, and even within this section, minor subnormal groups are responsible for a large proportion of the total number of cases'.

The dirt diseases such as scabies and impetigo will never be stamped out as long as there are neglected children. All kinds of vermin are transmitted from dirty homes to cleaner ones . . . The alarming spread of VD is taking place to large extent among girls of low morale who come from wretched and undisciplined homes. Not only prostitutes, but the homeless, unemployable youths and hardened tramps who form a considerable part of the chronic prison population are largely the product of the same kind of family. The case for the total eradication of this evil is overwhelming, and its abolition is a problem which must be tackled from many points . . . A large part of the solution will have to consist of personal treatment for the individual families, for these are pre-eminently the misfits who fail to benefit from the provisions which suffice for average people.

(Stephens, 1945, pp. 5—7)

Rarely has a year passed since 1945 when there has not been a report published which warns of the parasitical character of such families. The acuteness and depth of this concern is reiterated constantly in the annual reports of virtually every state social policy agency. According to the Department of Education and Science (1964), it is the children of these families who are the most disruptive in schools and the most ardent truants; reports from local housing departments identify these families as being the main arrears culprits and destroyers of property (Byrne, 1973); the DHSS have complained that these families not only form the long-term claimants but are the most time-consuming for their officers (Novak, 1978). And of course the observations of Dr Burt have been restated time and again, both within academic criminological circles (Wilson, 1966, p. 5; Carr Saunders *et al.*, 1943, p. 150) as well as the Home Office (1949, 1951), that it is the children from these families who form the majority of juvenile delinquents and adult criminals. In 1976 the Portia Trust, for example, gained considerable publicity with their claim that there existed within England and Wales 100,000 so-called criminal families who cost 'the state £10,000 a year ... these families are not particularly prone to hold gainful employment. It can be assumed that the majority live off the state in the form of social security benefits' (*The Sunday Times* 28 November 1976).

A further example can be found in the discussions concerning marriage breakdown. In the Working Party on Marriage Guidance document *Marriage Matters* (1979) there is repeated discussion about the high costs to the state and to the economy arising out of marriage breakdown. It is not a document which sympathetically discusses the human problems of those children and adults caught up in the tangles of a collapsing relationship. Similarly, the research committee of the Society of Conservative Lawyers has called for a Royal Commission on Marriage Breakdown largely because of the 'intolerable financial burden' occasioned by high divorce rates. And in evidence they cite the £800 million cost of supplementary benefits to one-parent families in 1978 and the cost of £180 million per annum occasioned by the children who have to come into 'care' due to marriage breakdown (*Financial Times* 11 May 1981, p. 5).

Virtually without exception it is possible to discover within every major official report or statement which discusses the social problems of clients a prevailing concern with the *costs* and the financial implications for the state's resources or capital's profits. All too often the issue of costs has been *one* of the major motive forces behind the state's increasing involvement in social reform. Although many writers of social policy and many leaders of social work have attempted to argue that the expansion of state social welfare has been the result of humanitarian impulses and deep concern over the plight of those human beings caught up in poverty (for a critique of these perspectives see Gettleman, 1974; Baker, 1979), the content of so many official reports and commissions points to a quite different set of motives.

WHY SOCIAL WORK INTERVENTION?

An important influence on the development and expansion of the personal social services, therefore, has been the manner in which social work became increasingly regarded as being one of the most appropriate strategies for reducing the problem of high-cost citizens. One central proposition, restated in successive official reports on social work, has been that social work forms of intervention are cheaper than institutional alternatives. To take just one example, the Seebohm Report noted that the reorganised personal social services should be able

> to prevent children having to be taken into care [and] would save heavy expenditure in other directions. The cost of keeping a child in a remand home is now £20 per week or over £1,000 per annum; the cost of keeping a child in an approved school is nearly as much, and the cost of keeping a child in a residential home is about £12 per week. A qualified social worker earns £1,060– £1,435 a year to which must be added the cost of supporting services. If an additional social worker can remove the need for two children coming into residential care the benefit to the community in terms of money is obvious.

(Seebohm Report, 1968, p. 16)

A further and vitally important ingredient of this cost—benefit argument which has been used to legitimise the expansion of social work has been the contention that social work offers the possibility of 'treatment'. In other words, it is not merely cheaper than institutional alternatives but more effective; it offers the promise that changes can be made in the ways that the residual poor live, and particularly in the manner in which they socialise their children. Thus by purporting to be one of the most promising strategies for breaking into the cycle of deprivation and of inculcating in clients a set of values which will permit them to be more self-reliant and capable of living without recourse to state resources, social work has promised long-term savings.

This was precisely what social work was offering. Throughout the 1950s and for most of the 1960s social work leaders were consistently and optimistically expounding the virtues of social work as being one of the most promising strategies for rehabilitating and controlling the hard-core poor (see Wootton, 1959). In this they were greatly assisted by the growing worries over the recurring high costs of institutionalisation and the evident failures of punitive and constraining methods to effect any significant change in the morality and behaviour of young offenders. Thus, where other state agencies had failed, or were just simply inappropriate, social work was being promoted as one of the most promising means for re-establishing a cheap and constructive relationship between 'society' and the 'deviant and nuisance' poor. The key to this effectiveness and promise of social work was identified as the personalised and gentle casework relationship established between the social worker and client, which was deemed to be the process through which those who seemingly lived beyond the norms, values and control of 'society' could be restored to 'normal' citizenship (McDougall and Cormack, 1954, p. 50). A glimpse of this process and its advantage over more traditional modes of control (for example, the 'banging of heads') was provided by an American social work writer discussing casework with juvenile offenders:

The great bulk of social work practice has internal change as its goal. Here we find that imposing, telling or giving orders does not work well. Only as the client is thoroughly involved and comes to accept on deepening levels the process of change can our methods be effective ... The delinquent can be forcibly placed in a training school, but he cannot be forced to change his notions of the kind of life he wants to lead. For this the inner boy must be involved, must decide to re-examine and to change. This is a very important reason for emphasising so much the significance of the relationship with the worker. Through it our boy learns to trust and to have confidence in the worker so that he can share some of his inward precious self with a view to change it. Only the boy can make this decision. Without his consent we can probably modify his outward behaviour; with it there is an opportunity for changes in inward values, an essential and basic purpose of social work.

(Bernstein, 1960, p. 8)

It was with such arguments that the supporters of social work pressed their case, and the benefits they so tantalisingly suggested were clearly impressive, promising massive savings in welfare spending and an important expansion in the supply of useful labour. Nevertheless, the state's expansion of social work cannot be solely attributed to the persuasiveness of the social work leadership. Equally important, if not more so, was the influence of those welfare state agencies already established and functioning.

As we have already noted, agencies such as education and social security were consistently complaining about the disproportionate costs and nuisance occasioned by a small number of individuals and families and the general intransigence of the problems. Many of these agencies came to argue that they did not have the capacity or the expertise to cope with these people and thereby actively supported the intervention of social workers and the expansion of state social work. For example, as early as 1949, the National Assistance Board in its Annual Report was complaining that

There are among the recipients of assistance a few 'problem families' of the kind which occupy the bulk of the time

of the workers, official and voluntary, in the field of
social maladjustment. The Board's officers have neither
the time to provide the almost continuous supervision
needed in these cases, nor the special skill which has to
be employed in effecting the education or re-education
of the parties if they are to lead acceptable lives . . . The
Board do not think that the provision of a general service
of moral rehabilitation is within their powers or duties.

(*Annual Report*, Cmd 8030, 1949, p. 18)

Similarly the British Medical Association was also lending
support in suggesting that while health visitors had many
skills to offer in work with problem families, that there were
many instances when 'the problem may be beyond her
ability to identify fully or deal with. Different techniques of
approach, analysis and guidance may be needed . . . and in
such situations the social caseworker has special advantages
of skill and tactical position' (Bristol BMA, 1959, p. 13). The
Department of Education and Science also gave periodic
support to the expansion and role of social work arguing that
children from problem families were particularly disruptive
of schools' functioning and that these children 'were a social
rather than an educational problem, and the teachers were
not equippped to meet it' (DES, 1964, p. 1).

The expansion and take-up of social work by successive
post-war governments did not thus simply reflect the success
of the social work profession to convince governments of its
legitimacy and value, but was also due to growing pressure
from many other welfare state agencies which were concerned
over the problems occasioned by a small group of the dependent poor and saw in social work a means of relieving the
burden. The pressure on government from these primary
welfare agencies was therefore a crucial factor in the growth
of state social work including the eventual reorganisation in
the early 1970s which made the referral of 'problem' patients,
children, tenants and claimants very much easier; it also gives
some indication of the subordinate servicing relationship
which has come to dominate the contact between the personal social services and these other parts of the state's welfare
system.

THE ELDERLY AND THE HANDICAPPED: THE
NUISANCE OF DEPENDENCY

Although not so obvious a nuisance and threat to the state as
problem families, there are the working-class elderly and
handicapped who now form a substantial section of social
work's client population. Social policy and social work
commentators have been content to explain this increase
primarily in demographic terms, noting correctly that the
proportion of the elderly in society has grown enormously
over the past twenty years. Obviously this is a factor, but
it is not a sufficient explanation for why so many should
end up as clients of social work.

A major reason why so many old and handicapped people
come to be clients centres on the issue of *dependency*, and
the problems that poses, not simply for the handicapped
and old themselves, but also for the state. To be old or handicapped in a capitalist society is immensely problematic for
those who have few independent resources and no wealth.
For both categories of people their chances of work are
virtually non-existent. Their labour power has either been
exhausted or is regarded, in the case of many handicapped
people, as being too difficult to exploit and extract. This is
particularly so in a period when labour is plentiful and
cheap. Thus these individuals are forced inevitably into a
position of dependency, for most working people can never
in the course of even a life of full-time work save enough
money to ensure an independent existence free from wage
labour. This burden of dependency has fallen in the past
seventy years jointly on the state (pensions and other benefits)
and the family of the pensioner or handicapped person.

For the state, the nuisance of dependency runs along two
main dimensions. First, the growing proportion of GNP
consumed by the old through benefits, pensions, beds in
long-stay hospitals, etc., runs contrary to one of the principal
objectives of capitalist policy, namely that the costs of
reproducing and maintaining labour should rest primarily
on the shoulders of the workers themselves through the
agency of the family. Second, the resources required and
used by the old and the handicapped cannot be regarded

from the viewpoint of profit accumulation as being a lucrative economic investment. It is an investment that yields very little directly in terms of economic growth and increased profits.

Therefore, from the standpoint of capital accumulation these sectors of the population tend to be regarded as parasitical. This sentiment was clearly stated by Robert Ensor, a liberal historian and a member of the influential Royal Commission on Population (1949), when he wrote that

> for the mainstay purposes of the nation, whether production in peace time or defence in war time, I am afraid that nearly all of them [the elderly] must be rated as passengers, not crew. Therefore, their enormous increase ... so far from mitigating the loss of those three million young adults [casualties of the war] actually makes it worse, since there is a much larger burden for the few shoulders to carry.
>
> (Ensor, 1950, p. 129)

Capitalism's narrow and inhuman way of understanding the place of the dependent old who have no opportunity for purchasing the care and attention available to the middle and upper classes has been reflected in the social policies which have been developed for them. It has been widely acknowledged that state pensions are inadequate even by governments who have done little to remove working-class pensioners and handicapped persons from having to claim (or not) means-tested supplementary benefits or rate and rent rebates. Indeed, there are now straws in the wind which indicate that pensions will not, even at their inadequate levels, be immune from the cuts in public spending. For according to Sir Geoffrey Howe, the Chancellor of the Exchequer, 'the increasing number of retired people in the population was adding to the cost of state spending on pensions, and those of working age should not have to bear an unsupportable burden' (cited in *The Times*, 13 May 1981).

Should the real value of pensions be further reduced, this would be entirely consistent with the recent drift of state social policies with respect to this section of the working-class population. The pressure on limiting public spending has done much to expose in greater clarity the increasing tendency of governments to resolve the nuisance of dependency by transferring the burden of care and support from the state to the family. This transfer, which has been under way for some time, features social work as one of the key agencies of its implementation. Under the grandiose title of 'community care', social work has for at least the past twenty-five years been concerned with removing the burden of dependency wherever possible from the state to that of the family. And whereas at the time of the Younghusband Report (1959) when such a policy was greeted as both 'sound economy as well as sound social policy' because it was certain 'to prove less costly than the alternatives of admission to residential care' (1959, para. 551), there was some degree of government support in the forms of home helps, domiciliary nursing and meals on wheel, recent cuts in these areas have starkly exposed the extent to which state policy has returned to the Victorian principles of familial responsibility with respect to the maintenance of dependants.

In terms of the weight of dependency, the brunt of caring has fallen with increasing acuteness upon the shoulders of women as daughters, wives or mothers rather than on the family as a whole. This role of women as principal carers of dependent relatives stretches back over many hundreds of years. However, due to working-class pressure at the beginning of the twentieth century (Collins, 1965) combined with a growing official awareness that limited state support could improve the capacity of families and particularly women to care for their elderly dependants, there has been a gradual expansion in welfare services for this sector of the population. This growth has now halted under the combined forces of economic depression and the Conservative government's belief that the expansion of state welfare had decisively weakened individual and familial responsibilities and duties. There has now been a decisive shift in responsibilities in which the state is rapidly withdrawing its already limited support to these vulnerable groups and thereby adding to the burden of a growing number of women who are compelled to care for their dependent relatives. This development was highlighted by a report published by the Equal Opportunities Commission (EOC) which investigated the carers of these groups:

> from the comments made in this survey [it was clear] that dependants — whether old, sick or handicapped — are not expected to require residential or domiciliary care when there is a female relative on hand. In general, assistance from the social services seems more likely to be available to dependants when their families are unable or unwilling to provide care, which on the face of things is understandable. The other side of the coin however is that many of the women who have retained the responsibility for a dependent relative do not receive the level of support which they really need. It is these women who pay the price.
>
> (EOC, 1980, p. 31)

This is the reality of community care. A policy which initially attracted widespread support because many saw it as a more humane and progressive alternative to dismal residential and institutional provision has for many resulted in the withdrawal of already inadequate state support. In common with many state social policies there has been a characteristic gulf between the rhetoric and the reality of the policy, typified in 1976 by the DHSS's *Priorities* document. At the very time this policy was being published, with its attractive catchphrase of 'putting people before buildings', the first rounds of major cuts were biting first and foremost into those services which were essential to the policy. And since that time the rundown in home helps, day centres, aids and adaptations has continued. With such a collapse in community services the local authority social services departments have been compelled to cajole a growing number of women and their families to shoulder the burden of looking after dependent relatives. Unfortunately for these dependants and their carers, the logic of capitalism brutally disregards the quality

of life for those who are marginal to the production processes
and lack political power and influence.

Social work has therefore become a significant form of
state 'intervention' in the lives of the dependent old and
handicapped poor, in the main because of their marginal
relationship to the labour market compounded by the
state's desire to limit increasingly the costs of their dependency. These factors, combined with lack of political power,
do seem to offer many insights and clues as to the nature of
social work intervention and practice with respect to this
significant segment of the client population: its low status; its
emphasis on familial self-help; its concern to prevent high-
cost institutionalisation, and a general lack of imagination
and commitment by the majority of social services departments to ensure that the experiences of ageing and handicap
are not humiliating and painful.

CONCLUSION

This chapter has a relatively simple conclusion: namely, that
the relationship of clients to the labour market is highly
significant in both defining an individual's client status and as
one of the determining forces shaping the styles and methods
of social work. This is an important conclusion if only because this labour dimension is far too often neglected within
many of the traditional discussions of clients. Within much
social policy writing as well as social work literature there is
often the tendency to explain the problematic status of clients
in psychologistic terms only, and a very common assertion
that the state's response is informed chiefly by feelings of
humanitarian benevolence. We have in Davies's *The Essential
Social Worker* (1981) an excellent example of such a por-
trayal of the state and social work. We are told, for example,
that 'the profession of social work is living testimony to a
political commitment to safeguard and further the welfare of
all citizens' (1981, p. 209). Unfortunately, explanations such
as these tend to distort the truth, which is far more brutal
and concerned with 'bottom-line' economic realities of
production, social costs, profits and, above all, with the capi-

talist logic which continually attempts to deal with human beings as commodity labour.

It is therefore necessary for those engaged in social work to try to make more clear just what is involved. There are many misconceptions about the character of social work and its client population. This is in part due to the class-specific character of much social work practice, for unlike other primary areas of the welfare state such as education, health and even housing and social security the personal social services tend only to touch a small minority of the population: a minority, moreover, who tend to be marginal to most key areas of social life including the labour market, the organised labour movement, political parties, and vast areas of cultural activity. Indeed, isolation and loneliness are common to many clients.

This marginality of the bulk of the client population has many consequences, some of which are discussed in detail in Chapter 4. One of the most obvious is that the non-client population tends to have little direct experience of social work or the personal social services, which can mean that they are unable to test the authenticity of the opinions which are generated about this activity and its recipients, whether these are generated in the mass media or within their own cultural networks. One such opinion which has a degree of strength is that the personal social services are involved with 'welfare'. The reactions to this opinion are varied, but at a very general level it is not uncommon to find that some people regard this welfare as 'bad' when it is applied to young offenders or problem families — 'they take advantage'; 'they need a harder line', etc. — and 'good' when it is applied to old or handicapped people. Both of these general positions need to be challenged.

Taking the latter position (as the other is discussed later) the problem is that by its very existence social work seems to support the view that 'something is being done' for the dependent old and handicapped. It also tends to legitimate a view that the state is genuinely concerned about the plight of this most vulnerable section of the community. To some degree these views are supported by the evidence; at least workhouses have been withdrawn, and many social workers are genuinely helpful and thoughtful. Given these contradictions, it is not sufficient simply to criticise services for the elderly or handicapped poor on the basis of inadequacy of provision. These criticisms have rarely had any dramatic impact on radically changing the service, and in the particular context of cuts the likelihood of them being pushed to one side is even greater.

One of the purposes of this chapter in identifying such factors as the relationship of clients to the labour market, and the problematic of dependency to capitalism, has been to suggest the kind of criticisms and perspectives which go beyond issues of provision, amount and access to resources and provisions. For while these immediate problems should never be ignored — if they were, then there could possibly be even further cutbacks and even poorer provision — the domain assumptions and values which shape the ways in which those who have a marginal relationship to wage labour and production are treated and regarded need to be challenged. Thus, with respect to the elderly and handicapped, their low-priority status within the client population, the manner in which they have experienced a disproportionate degree of the cutbacks in public spending, the fact that social work intervention, if any, tends to be infrequent and often inadequate; that resources and provisions within all branches of state social policy tend to be similarly underdeveloped and poorly supported, these all reflect their diminished status as labour. Links should continually be made between the the paucity of the welfare services for the old and handicapped, the style of social welfare directed at problem families and juvenile delinquents, and the wider issues relating to the immoral economy of capitalism.

Social workers are in a particularly advantageous position to undertake this kind of linking work. Many are genuinely moved by the plight of clients, and struggle daily to extract as much as possible from often grudging welfare agencies. But it is doubtful whether social workers alone will be able to transform those values so central to capitalism, that those who are not engaged in productive wage labour and who have grave problems in maintaining their independence are less worthy human beings. But social workers can make an enormous contribution in demonstrating that it is this value system in particular which is so important for determining the major parameters within which social work and social welfare policies operate.

Finally, in stressing the importance of the labour dimension as a crucial factor in the formation of state social work and its client population, the limitations of this 'economistic' concept as the sole determining influence on social work should be realised. It is undoubtedly an important factor but it is not the only one. If economic considerations such as the potential for labour or the costs of dependency were the only key influences on the development and nature of social work, then it would be hard to see how social work could ever be considered a contradictory activity. Certainly, the practice implications of a social work activity based solely on economistic foundations would be relatively unproblematic; it would also tend to be far more brutal than it is in reality. For the pure doctrine of labour potential would undoubtedly condemn the majority of the working-class old and handicapped to the most dire circumstances with a total withdrawal and absence of state resources, other than perhaps some type of euthanasia service to bring about the easy end demanded by the withdrawal from production.

Even though the social policy strategy of Margaret Thatcher's government is probably the nearest to such an 'economistic' version that Britain has experienced for over fifty years, the history of post-war social work development and expansion suggests that there have been other influences that have operated alongside, and at times in tension with the more narrow economistic concerns. Among the most important of these has been the influence of social democracy and working-class pressure, which are explained in the next chapter in order to assess their impact on shaping the development of social work.

3
Clients and Social Democracy

THE SPIRIT OF 1945

Although many of those who became clients of the expanding personal social services were often marginal to and neglected by organised labour — this point is discussed in detail in the next chapter — they were nevertheless directly affected by the demand for fundamental social change made during and immediately after the Second World War by the labour movement. And even if there has been more fragmentation of the working class since that time, due in part to the operation of welfare itself, there was then at least some degree of understanding and consensus that some of the problems of clients were quite evidently the result of gross patterns of structural inequality and inadequate welfare provision which had affected large sections of the unemployed throughout the inter-war period.

This pressure did not simply focus on the level and quantity of services, but also on the style and quality of provision. After the bitterness of the inter-war depression, and especially the cruel policies of poor relief, the labour movement was determined to bring about not only more welfare but a better form of welfare that did not humiliate and stigmatise those who needed help. A particular goal of organised labour in this respect was the demand to reduce the extent of means-testing within income-maintenance policies, and the formation of a health service which not only provided care free at the point of delivery but was also democratically controlled.

In 1945 the labour movement was tremendously excited by its crushing electoral victory over the Tories, and aspirations were running high for a Parliament in which Labour had such a dominating majority. This is how Gallacher, a Communist Party MP at the time, described the scenes in the House of Commons:

What a House. Nearly 400 Labour MPs [384], most of them new and all eager and anxious to get down to the job. Such fire, such enthusiasm. They were on top of the world. They had the Tories down and they meant to keep them down. They cheered and laughed and roared. When the Tories, conscious of defeat and dreading what might be before them tried to make a demonstration on the entrance of Churchill, they met with a response from the Labour benches that just about frightened them out of their wits. For the first time they heard within the 'sacred precincts' the stirring chorus of the *Red Flag*.

(Gallacher, 1951, pp. 17–18)

As is well known – although perhaps the lessons have not yet been fully learnt – the parliamentary power of the Labour party did not bring about the new world of socialism. So many of the reforms demanded by the organised working class were never realised, and those that did emerge did so heavily amended and compromised. The health service, for example, although an important step forward, was never placed under the desired democratic control and neither did it emerge with health centres as one of its central features, a point that had been stressed by Bevan (*Hansard*, 30 April 1946, cols 57–8) as being essential for an efficient socialist health service. Similarly, the much heralded Beveridge plan for income-maintenance services was substantially modified and weakened on such essential points as levels of subsistence and rights to national insurance benefits for the entire duration of unemployment or sickness by the time it reached the statute books.

The failure of the Labour government to represent the aspirations and hopes of working people despite its massive majority in Parliament and a clear mandate for fundamental radical change clearly signals the power of capital. It was not just that the actual process of drawing up the legislation was left 'in the hands of civil servants and professionals, whose class bias, particularly in the upper echelons, remained unshaken' (Ginsburg, 1979, p. 9), though that was important, but that the decision of the Labour government under immense pressure to ally with the Americans over Marshall Aid (which was in essence a decision of West European capitalist countries to yield to the power and influence of American capital) critically set and limited some of the parameters for subsequent post-war reconstruction (Gallacher, 1951, ch. 7).

Certainly during the 1945–51 Labour administration the effects of this alliance of subordination were evident in both foreign (e.g. over Greece) and domestic policy. One has a sense of continuity reading of the devaluation debacle in 1949, and of the pressure on the British economy to meet its American commitments with the inevitable round of cuts in capital expenditure. The cuts, needless to say, created havoc for the social welfare commitments of the Labour government. Housing, education, social services and health were yet again major casualties of a so-called inevitable and unavoidable economic crisis.

Nevertheless, despite these qualifications, certain significant gains were achieved through the emergence of a more vigorous brand of social democracy. One tangible gain for working people was in the improved *access* to a wide range of state services – health, education, public housing and social security. (As the Education Group of the Centre for Contemporary Cultural Studies has noted, the 'politics of access' was particularly prevalent within the Labour Party, and still is, and unfortunately came to be seen as 'enough' (1981, p. 64) to the detriment of a concern over quality and style of service.) Less tangible, although by no means less significant, was the influence of social democracy in bringing about a markedly changed atmosphere in terms of the manner in which a wide range of social problems and social issues were discussed. It was this changed atmosphere that was to have particular importance for the post-war growth of social work.

A CHANGED ATMOSPHERE

This change in atmosphere was brought about through the interaction of numerous factors during the immediate post-war period. Social democratic writers, and politicians in particular, came to regard groups such as problem families and the poor concentrated in inner-city areas as major black-spots in the push towards the 'new civilisation' of a high-employment mixed economy with a caring welfare state. From social policy theorists such as Titmuss to Labour politicians such as Crosland one of the crucial tests of the progressive quality of social democracy became the extent to which these hard-core pockets of poverty and despair could be eliminated by becoming absorbed into the general movement of prosperity that characterised post-war Britain. In the words of Titmuss, 'the attributes that society adopts to its deviants, and especially its poor and politically in-articulate deviants, reflects its ultimate values' (1957, p. v).

The heightened concern for these sections of the working-class poor did signal a marked change in the ways in which they were discussed and understood, with subsequent impli-cations for policy. Although the legislation enacted can be criticised (with good reason), the importance of the changes which took place should not be underestimated, and neither should the genuine desire of social democratic writers and politicians to implement legislation which attempted to help and assist the residual and previously stigmatised poor be dismissed. Thus to a considerable degree the plight of this group began to be considered far more sensitively than hitherto with a degree of compassion unheard of before the war.

The principle of *universalism*, for example, embodied in the National Health Service Act, National Insurance Act, Family Allowances Act and Education Act epitomised this shift in attitudes. As Titmuss argued:

One fundamental historical reason for the adoption of this principle was the aim of making services available and accessible to the whole population in such ways as would not involve users in any humiliating loss of status, dignity or self-respect. There should be no sense of inferiority, pauperism, shame or stigma in the use of a publicly provided service; no attribution that one was being or becoming a 'public burden'. Hence the emphasis on the social rights of all citizens to use or not to use as responsible people the services made available by the community which the private market and the family were unable or unwilling to provide universally.

(Titmuss, 1968, p. 129)

The importance of this political and ideological change of attitude can be further illustrated when the manner in which those who became clients before the war is considered. What we find is that for over a hundred years and more those who came to constitute the bulk of modern social work's clientele had been the subject of a most damning and punitive set of welfare practices and ideologies. The Charity Organisation Society (COS), which was established in 1869 in London, rapidly expanded throughout Britain and had a decisive influence would never, for example, willingly become involved with many of those who eventually became clients of state social work on the grounds that they were so morally bankrupt and inadequate that they were unhelpable through such strategies as rehabilitative casework (Jones, 1978, ch. 3). Indeed, according to the COS leadership, any strategy which sought to assist the undeserving poor through the provision of material aid of any sort and amount was not only doomed to failure, but would actually make the situation worse by providing the means for their reproduction. Thus, according to Bernard Bosanquet of the COS, the very idea that 'something must be done'

is in and by itself a potent factor in the creation of the miserable class whose existence we deplore; and all attempts to palliate the mischief by twining ropes of sand in pretending to organise the unorganisable material simply aggravate the disease by furnishing that partial and discontinuous employment which is the poison that corrupts these people's lives.

(Bosanquet, 1895, pp. 113—14)

Even the more liberal sections of the reform intelligentsia at the turn of the twentieth century, such as the Fabian Society, shared with the COS this perspective that the best social policy for these sections of the poor was systematic neglect in the hope (inspired by Social Darwinism) that they could be prevented from reproduction (Harris, 1972; Stedman Jones, 1971).

Thus when intervention was recommended the proposals were nearly always of the most punitive kind. The objective was not rehabilitation but containment and eradication. This was particularly well stated by Whetham, a eugenicist, in 1909:

In dealing with men and women of this character where we cannot hope to accomplish individual radical cure, we must, as with the feeble-minded, organise the extinction of the tribe. In the old days the law attempted this extinction by hanging, a preventative of the sternest and most efficient nature . . . For us, the old methods are impossible. We must attain the same result by the longer and gentler system of perpetual segregation in detention colonies and with all the mitigations that are practicable.

(Whetham, 1909, pp. 214—15)

Right up to the outbreak of war in 1939 the demand for the state to act in such a way that it actively contained and controlled the reproduction and life-chances of the undeserving poor (also called the 'residuum', the 'stagnant' and, more recently, 'problem families') was shared by social reformers from the liberal left to the conservative right. Moreover, successive social policies had built into their administration discriminatory clauses which ensured that certain benefits were withheld from those considered as 'disreputable'. Such clauses were to be found in many of the welfare reforms enacted by the 1906 Liberal administration, including old-age pensions and national insurance benefits.

SOCIAL DEMOCRACY AND SOCIAL WORK

Given that social work was changing significantly during the inter-war period and, under the growing influence of Freudian ideas, was coming to believe that positive rehabilitative work was possible with the residuum, the need to reduce the dominance of earlier negative and repressive attitudes was critical to the possibility of social work's development as a major welfare state strategy. Theories of biological and genetic determinism which legitimise many of the hostile attitudes to the non-productive and deviant poor clearly offered no prospect of rehabilitative, social, work. Rather, they pointed to the necessity of containment and studied neglect as being the only sure ways of ridding society of such problems.

Within academic and professional circles, especially criminology (Taylor, et al., 1973), the advent of the more progressive treatment-orientated theories provoked profound debates. Indeed, the arguments over this nature/nurture dichotomy continue, particularly over racial disadvantage. However, that the more liberal rehabilitative perspectives as epitomised by psychodynamics and social work emerged to exercise such influence over the development of the post-war welfare state cannot be attributed solely to some resolution of those debates in favour of the 'nurture' camp. Rather, the struggle of the working class to implement a more vigorous social democratic politics throughout the 1930s culminating in the Labour victory in 1945 was the decisive turning-point. For it was a central feature and theme of this politics that the problems besetting the majority of the working-class poor lay in the structure and organisation of society rather than in their 'biology'. Moreover, whether it was in the obvious areas of income maintenance or in health, organised labour was demanding a change in the *style* of state welfare policy, moving away from the repressive and dehumanising style of policies such as the Poor Law. As Donzelot has argued, such pressure was an important feature in pressing the state to develop strategies such as social work with its psychoanalytic perspectives. For

> While law, medicine, psychiatry, and religion did provide techniques for managing conflictual relations and malad-justments, virtually all of these techniques implied heavy-handed solutions involving direct constraint and hence a high cost in terms of resistance to their application. In contrast, psychoanalysis supplies – directly or indirectly – responses of a regulatory and non-coercive type.
>
> (Donzelot, 1979, p. xxiv)

This social democratic politics was immensely significant therefore for the re-emergence of social work after the Second World War. Although it was primarily articulated and supported by the organised working class, it did provide the ideological climate for the more liberal and humane welfare theories and practices to be extended to the un-organised and impoverished dependent poor. Their impact should not be underestimated, despite the fact that many of these 'new' strategies continued to maintain a primary focus upon the individual rather than on the structural processes affecting power and human well-being. For, while many social workers have rightly become circumspect about how they understand state social work's vocabulary of 'love', 'self-determination' and 'acceptance' when referring to clients, it is important to remember that such terms had never been applied earlier to the 'undeserving' residual poor who now comprised such a large section of the client population. Indeed, the very idea that the residuum had emotions or feelings worthy of respect and consideration was anathema to many past social reformers. Similarly, the idea that they could be restored to active citizenship through a caring strategy of casework and re-education would have been considered outrageous. As Lawrance of the Family Welfare Association (the new name from 1946 of the COS) remarked, 'In the past, the families who today we are trying to treat with special concern and are calling problem families were probably written off as "poor law cases" or "feckless and unhelpful"' (1950, p. 1).

However, the new psychologistic and psychodynamic approaches to the problems of poverty and deviancy offered many apparent advantages to the state. These liberal strategies promised both success and cheapness in the form of restoration to active citizenship and self-reliance, thereby reducing dependency on the recently expanded state resources. Similarly, many of the central tenets of these practices and theories remained entirely congruent with prevailing attitudes concerning the primacy of the family and the sanctity of private property just as they continued to blame the victims for their plight.

These important qualifications should not detract from the crucial role played by the working class in pushing the state towards more liberal and extensive welfare policies. Unfortunately, as has happened so many times in the past, working-class pressure was decisive in forcing the pace of change but failed to control the state agencies which emerged to implement the subsequent reforms. Instead, as the case of state social work exemplifies, post-war social democracy (even under Atlee) did not permit the popular control of welfare services, insisting instead upon the rule of experts and professionals. This anti-democratic strand and accompanying distrust of popular democracy is a particular feature of liberal social democracy and is undoubtedly one of the principal factors which explains why so much of the radical and working-class intent behind the demands for the extension and humanisation of state social policy was only partially realised.

A WORKING-CLASS GAIN?

To what extent, therefore, can the emergence and subsequent growth of state social work since the Second World War be considered a gain for the working class and for clients? A clear-cut and unambiguous answer is not possible. Rather, social work's development points to it being a peculiarly dynamic and contradictory state activity in which many of its methods and theories can be used along a wide continuum that has repressive objectives at one end and more liberal and

humane possibilities at the other. Indeed, it is this very complex range of opportunities within social work which makes
it such a difficult activity for the state, clients and social
workers.

For many clients, this problematic character of social
work does give rise to considerable confusion and uncertainty.
In a recent article, 'What the Client Thinks of You', Kitchen
(1980) reported on a wide range of divergent attitudes among
clients: some were bemused — 'What was the social worker
doing here . . . she came in every week for about three hours
and she just used to sit there and say nothing, nothing at all';
others, particularly the isolated elderly and handicapped
were tremendously positive — 'She was a great help. She kept
coming every week to talk. She was a real good pal . . . what
would I have done without her?'; and then there were those
who were deeply critical — 'She says one thing when she's
here and another when she's back at the Social Services with
the rest of them'; or as another single mother reported (fifteen
years as a 'case' and twelve different social workers):

> Then my house was broken into, and they even took the
> cooker. I phoned up the welfare and asked if they could
> help me get money for a second-hand cooker so I could
> keep the family together. But no, instead they took the
> children into care until I could raise the money for the
> cooker, which cost them more money in the long run. And
> while the children were in care they managed to run away
> and nobody knew where they'd gone. After that I knew I
> couldn't trust the welfare again.
>
> (Kitchen, 1980)

These reflections illuminate just how varied are the clients'
experiences of social work and social workers, and the presence
of a broad spectrum of possibilities within this part of state
social welfare. (If more evidence was available from the clients
themselves, then undoubtedly one would be in a better
position to judge the potential of social work, and to devise
fruitful lines of action.)

In the absence of this evidence from clients the pre-
dominance of third-party referrals indicates at least a degree

of hesitancy on the part of potential clients to become involved with the personal social services. What referral patterns tend to suggest is that there is a substantial degree of unevenness in client attitudes towards the personal social services. On the one hand, it appears there is client demand (and self-referral) for the provision of services — nursery places, aids and adaptations, bus passes, home helps, meals on wheels, etc. And the investigations of Goldberg *et al.* (1970) indicate a degree of satisfaction, especially from the elderly, when such services are provided. Given that the cuts have ravaged this area of service provision in particular, it is more than likely that future research will indicate frustration and unhappiness. But on the other hand, and this is hardly surprising, referral patterns do suggest a degree of resistance by clients in areas such as child care, family and debt problems, where the referral agent tends to be an official body of one sort or another. It is hardly surprising that many working people are deeply reluctant to involve state officials in these private parts of their lives and are similarly anxious about the powers of social workers to, say, remove children and generally take over responsibility for their own lives.

The sensitivity of social work to the provision of material aid also indicates the qualified manner in which the break with past punitive policies has been realised. Within social work itself there have been profound divisions concerning the degree of liberality and compassion to be shown to clients. In his work on policies towards homeless families, for example, Minns (1972) discovered that social workers employed in the pre-Seebohm welfare departments were far more likely to take a punitive view of homelessness as compared with child-care officers in the children's departments. Minns, in accounting for these differences, suggested that training was a possible factor in that the workers in the welfare department dealing with homelessness were not professionally qualified social workers, whereas in the children's department over half of the staff were (1972, p. 5). However, as Minns further suggested, the difference between the two social work agencies would appear to lie more in the continuing influence of the Poor Law ideology of less eligibility within the welfare department as against the liberal treatment perspectives of the children's department rather than as a simple function of training.

It is still the case that in many areas of social work a deep stream of suspicion can be sensed towards particular client groups which is reflected in part in the discussions about client manipulation of social workers which figures in much of the literature.

HOLISM AND THE PROGRESSIVE POTENTIAL OF SOCIAL WORK

Despite the attempts to modify in practice social work's humanitarian principles, the recent history of social work demonstrates that by their very presence and assertion these principles have allowed social workers to undertake practice which can at times conflict with some of the central features of bourgeois ideology, provoking considerable tensions and many unintended consequences for the state, and achieving some worthwhile gains for clients.

For example, progressive social workers have been able to use these principles to justify a wide range of strategies with clients that protect them from some of the harsher aspects of state policy. By drawing on their insights of clients' lives that comes from adopting a more holistic approach, many social workers have been able to marshal evidence to persuade a reluctant state agency to be more liberal and sensitive in its approach. In the area of juvenile justice, for example, many social workers have been successful in keeping a young offender out of penal institutions by pre- senting a social enquiry report in which the client's history has been used to justify a less extreme and more humane alternative.

It is the *holistic* style of social work that establishes one of its profoundly contradictory characteristics. For although deeply qualified, social work is almost unique among state activities in the extent to which it regards the residual poor as human beings with feelings and emotions. In this respect contemporary social work is markedly different from previous strategies directed at the undeserving poor in which the state showed very little concern for the client's history, the stresses of poverty and poor housing or intra-familial tensions.

Thus, no matter how deformed the interaction between some social workers and clients may become, it is almost unique among state interventions in this section of the population in the extent to which it considers a wide range of interrelating issues affecting people both now and in the past. While these issues — whether related to housing, education, employment, fuel, poverty, isolation, marriage breakdown, or whatever — may be the site of conflict between social workers and clients, or social workers and their managers, as to what they signify, that they are considered at all as factors influencing a person's life marks a crucial gain when it is noted that a general tendency of capitalism is to abstract human experiences into a series of discrete and unconnected fragments. Thus although social work practice too often fails to be holistic, the potential remains. It continues to be an avowed principle of social work practice and theory (and was confirmed as such by the Barclay Committee) which can be exploited with immediate effect to clients' benefit and with wider political consequences in the construction of more convincing and accurate accounts of the multiplicity of pressures that affect clients.

TENSIONS WITHIN THE STATE

Even in its partial implementation by contemporary state social work the principle of holism has created many problems for the state. This is well illustrated in the controversy concerning social work's role with juvenile delinquents and the debate over the 1969 Children and Young Persons Act. The police, for example, who have become especially critical of the influence of social work in the control of juvenile delinquency, have found social workers' concern with the wider issues relating to a youngster's delinquency particularly irksome. Whereas the police — and this is shared by many magistrates — are primarily concerned with the crime itself, social work maintains that this is merely a symptom of a greater problem. Depending on the particular style of the social worker, reasons varying from family relationships to those concerning the particular environment of working-class youths are put forward as explanations of delinquency. These in turn can have a considerable influence over how the young offender will be dealt with, and in some instances can protect the youngster from the more punitive and penal aspects of the legal system. According to the police, and many others, this more holistic approach of social work has led to many youngsters being able 'to get away with' delinquent actions. Typical of the kind of outrage expressed by the police at this development was the statement of the then Deputy Chief Constable of West Yorkshire who exclaimed that the police were 'Fed up with the softly, softly, namby-pamby pussyfooting approach to the vicious elements who have never had it so good . . . The social services . . . should be taken out of the criminal scene altogether' (*Daily Telegraph*, 19 May 1976).

This sort of antagonism is also evident in social work's relationship with other state agencies. Fuel boards, housing authorities and social security offices are among those which find social work's more holistic approach to clients problematic. Again, these agencies operate along more restrictive lines than does social work, preferring to deal only with specific and narrow aspects of an individual's life: for example, their tenancy, their ability to meet bills or manage on benefits. Social workers, on the other hand, when dealing with clients who have been referred by these agencies because of some specific problem, tend to take a wider view. They attempt to discover, for example, why a client should be in arrears or debt, and in doing so often include the manner in which the referring agency undertakes its work as part of the problem.

Thus it is not uncommon to find many social workers expressing serious reservation and criticisms of other state agencies as being in part responsible for the client's problems. It is well known that many social workers are deeply critical of the way in which social security offices handle the problems of their clients and it is not unusual to find that many social workers regard social security officers as being too insensitive and inflexible to their clients' needs.

Not surprisingly, this has led to considerable antagonism between the two agencies (Leach, 1981). In their report on the supplementary benefits organisation, Spender and Crookston (1978) discovered that many SB officers regarded social workers as 'do-gooders who are too emotionally involved and hence are easily taken in by false stories'.

Very often tensions of this type are rooted in the clash of perspectives between the two agencies. Whereas social security organisations are primarily concerned with a claimant's entitlement to benefits, social workers are involved with the broader aspects of a claimant's circumstances and situation and are more directly aware of the problems caused by the complex bureaucracy of the DHSS and the effect of the more abrupt and stigmatising social relationships embodied in this part of the state on their clients.

Another major area where such tensions have increasingly bubbled to the surface has been with regard to the fuel boards. As the price of fuels has rocketed, more and more clients have faced difficulties in paying their bills, which in turn have often been compounded by wholly inadequate and expensive heating systems installed in many council-owned houses. Given that benefit levels have not risen to take account of these rising costs, many social workers are now spending a considerable part of their working day attempting to help clients meet their bills and avoid disconnection.

Thus the fuel boards have suffered complaints from social workers, who have brought to their attention the consequences of their policies, and the many interconnecting problems facing clients in meeting their obligations. Indeed, it was largely due to the pressure of social services departments that the fuel boards were forced to depart slightly from their narrow commercial approach and agree to a code of conduct concerning the disconnections of particularly vulnerable consumers — the old, and families with young children in particular. Although such a shift has not dramatically improved the situation of fuel poverty for many clients, and many fuel boards have sought to circumvent the codes of conduct, it was nevertheless a partial victory which has brought limited relief to some clients.

It should also be noted that the holistic approach of

social work also attracts the wrath of some state agencies, and conservative opinion generally, due to the seemingly permissive style which such a welfare strategy demands from social workers. The holistic mode of social work, requiring detailed and often intimate information relating to a client's life, demands a personalised and 'softly-softly' approach by the social workers. This is the only way in which the client's trust can be gained and an environment created in which the client will yield revealing personal insights. Thus brusqueness and punitive and judgemental attitudes are inappropriate attitudes for social workers in that they tend to defeat the possibility of developing the all-important 'treatment' relationship with a client. This style of work has enraged those who believe that social workers should be uncompromising in telling their clients why they are a nuisance and be firm in their work of controlling them. As Rhodes Boyson has argued:

> Too many people in charge of the morals of our young have been brainwashed by mindless sociologists. They give no guidance, no standards, no discipline. We need more policemen and fewer social workers. Social workers are becoming part of the trouble with Britain.
>
> (cited in Pearson, 1978, p. 19)

That such tensions exist between social services departments and other state and official agencies does highlight the contradictory position of the personal social services as a servicing/dustbin agency of the welfare state. On the one hand, the primary welfare agencies welcome the presence of social workers who can pick up their time-consuming and difficult cases, as was discussed earlier, but on the other hand, they do not like it when those social workers begin to question and criticise the referral agencies' policies and practices, or bring to light information and details which cannot be dealt with by their bureaucratic procedures.

PROGRESSIVE FEATURES

It is possible to list many examples of social workers in conflict with other state agencies, but the point here is that many of these tensions stem from the particular progressive features within social work that make it an activity worthy of attention and defence. These progressive features include the possibility within social work for understanding the problems and circumstances of clients in a more holistic fashion than is possible in other state welfare activities; it also includes the potential for a more humane consideration of clients which is often at odds with much prevailing opinion concerning significant sections of the client population such as problem families and delinquents, where punitive and stigmatising ideology and theory are still rife. Both of these combine in turn to permit certain dominant attitudes to be challenged. Social work allows for perspectives that are not simply shaped and determined by economistic and commercial considerations, and that include a consideration of human needs, emotions and feelings, factors that have so often been ignored with respect to the residual, non-productive sections of the population. In this sense, such fragments of anti-capitalist logic cause enormous internal problems for social work and are not simply present in the sometimes fraught intra-state agency contacts. Indeed much of the toughening-up process currently under way in social work is a product of such internal strains: the clash between the more compassion-ate approach which takes account of human needs and feelings with the conflicting demand on social work to reduce the costs and nuisances of the non-productive, surplus poor.

More generally, evidence of these tensions does counteract that view of the state which has some currency on the Left, which posits the state as an all-powerful homogeneous entity which is remorselessly efficient, co-ordinated and effective in pursuing the interest of capital. This view of the state, as Paul Corrigan (1977, p. 88) has argued, has appalling political consequences. One such consequence is to relegate the working class to being nothing more than passive onlookers in the process of social development. Social welfare policy and history also becomes nothing more than the evidence of the power of capital to manipulate people successfully in its interest. And for the many people who are now employed by the state, there can be no possibility for progressive action and struggle. The kinds of tensions discussed in this chapter are crucial in providing evidence that capital and the state are not omnipotent. Moreover, the tensions and contradictions within the state are clearly more than mere bureaucratic or organisational inconsistencies within a complex system. Rather, they reflect very real and long-standing conflicts concerning the welfare of working people, and demonstrate the manner in which the state has become an actual site of the struggle between capital and labour, in which one of the central if not always explicit battles has been over the fight of working people to gain the right to be treated as human beings.

Thus, whereas state social work is by no means a socialist activity, neither is it always entirely consistent with capitalist logic. Indeed, for all the major participants of social work — the state, clients and social workers — it is a difficult and contradictory activity, bringing with it advantages and disadvantages for all groups. For the clients, as the earlier quotations made clear, social work can bring either relief or further anxiety. Very often, what is understood as being progressive aspects of social work, such as its more compassionate and holistic approach, are experienced by clients as oppressive and mystifying, and allow for ever-deeper penetration by the state in their lives. Thus, where the police dislike the 'softly-softly' approach of social workers and the way in which they take crime as a symptom of deeper personal problems, so for the delinquents this approach can also be deeply problematical when it means that for the most minor of offences they could find themselves on the end of indeterminate 'in-care' sentences (cf. Matza, 1969). In a similar fashion the holism of traditional social work has been deformed by a psychologistic approach that makes it especially qualified and conditional. The concern with a client's history and emotions is often impelled by the search for individual personality factors which are considered to explain why a client is a nuisance, different, and a problem to the state; its holism is partial and double-edged, for social work itself operates its own set of fragmentary categories into which it seeks to place clients — the welfare zoo made up of the different cages into which the clients are allocated. This does much to disguise the class character of social work and its specific focus on the working-class poor.

Nevertheless, the potential for socialists and radicals within social work are considerable. It is not so much a question of vanguardism, for neither social workers nor clients are likely to be the main catalysts of a socialist revolution. Yet both are in a position to make a substantial contribution to the struggle for a better society and to the immediate day-to-day politics of the working class. Some of the best critics of the welfare state who have seen through the ideology of the caring state can be found among clients, some of whom have a view from below of a massive range of state agencies and activities and a corresponding experience second to none. Moreover, some of these clients do not have to be told about the problems of reformism or the inadequacies of social democracy, and many did not need to be told that the great problem with state welfare was not so much the quantity (although it is often a problem) but the quality, i.e. the oppressive and stigmatising way in which state welfare is administered.

Social workers are themselves in a strategic position of considerable sensitivity to the state. They, too, from their different perspective gain an unparalleled view of the state in action; they, too, can see the sorts of problems that are created by these state forms and the immense toll which many capitalist processes exert on clients. There are few state workers such as social workers who inhabit as their primary domain these nether regions of society, and who can gain at first hand some insight into problems and circumstances which the state would like to minimise and hide.

4

Clients and the Working Class

INTRODUCTION

We now set out to explore the nature and implications of the relationships which exist between clients and those other sections of the working class who have no contact with social workers and social services departments. In particular this chapter attempts to come to terms with the often strained and antagonistic feelings that at times characterise relations between clients and the 'respectable' working class. This has constituted one of the barriers to a united working-class response to some of the issues and problems confronting the poor.

First, it is shown how some of the tensions and strains which characterise the position of the residual and surplus poor within the working class are rooted in the material experiences of working-class life. Then the manner in which they have been acted upon and exacerbated by state social policies concerning social work and the mass media is explored. Finally, an alternative theoretical framework based on the work of Marx and Engels is constructed in order to suggest some of the possibilities for action which would help overcome the isolation of clients from the organised working class.

STRAINS WITHIN THE WORKING CLASS

Although there is very little material which examines the relationship of clients to the organised sections of the working

class, there is sufficient evidence to suggest that certain segments of the client population such as problem families and
juvenile delinquents have a particularly marginal and strained
status in the eyes of the 'respectable' working population.
Coates and Silburn (1970), for example, in their influential
work on St Annes in Nottingham, discovered that problem
families, delinquents, tramps and the like were stigmatised
heavily by their more respectable neighbours. Means (1977)
likewise noted that problem families were regarded as a grave
nuisance by many neighbours and considered to be one of
the main reasons for lowering the image of their working-class
neighbourhood. Indeed, one could go much further back in
history to show well-entrenched strands of criticism within
organised labour's politics and culture towards sections of
the residual poor population. While it may not be so surprising to discover that prominent Fabians at the end of the
last century were committed to social-relief policies that dif-
ferentiated between the 'genuine' unemployed and the so-
called 'loafers' and 'idlers' (e.g. Oakeshott' 1894, p. 9), the
Labour party also had a most guarded attitude towards the
'undeserving poor' and did not regard them as suitable and
acceptable targets of their politics. Ramsay MacDonald,
for example, claimed in 1908 that the Labour party 'never
willingly touch a slum population, or one that has shown
no signs of intelligent initiative, like trade unionism and
co-operation' (*Nineteenth Century*, vol. 63, p. 343).

THE PROBLEM OF CLIENTS

The strained and often stigmatised position of significant
sections of the client population within the working class
constitutes one of the most important problems confronting
radical and progressive social workers, and has a considerable
bearing on the nature of working-class politics. It can be
shown that a great deal of the antagonism which exists
between some client groups and other sections of the working
class rests on actual material experiences and circumstances
that are quite different from the myths that are expressed
towards them within state policy and by the bourgeoisie.

Many social workers will be aware that some of their clients are not only problems for the state, for the reasons examined in previous chapters, but also for their neighbours and immediate community. The victims of many juvenile delinquents are, for example, too often working people who can ill afford to lose property or have it vandalised. Similarly there are those families who have little control over their children who are regarded with disdain because their children can be a nuisance, often more so in high-density working-class housing estates or blocks of flats where play-space is either inappropriate or absent. In these particular instances the actions of social services departments themselves can exacerbate these intra-class tensions. For those neighbours who have been inconvenienced by living next door to a family whose house is deteriorating, whose children are noisy until the early hours of the morning, and so on and so forth, the sight of seeing a social worker visiting can be a cause of outrage. This outrage can be compounded if they see the social worker delivering 'goodies' (e.g. furniture) of one sort or another or arranging special programmes and treats for the youngsters, as their own material circumstances may be little better than that of the neighbours who receive such help. Their survival independent of the help of state agencies may be, and often is, very difficult and hard. Yet there is no public acknowledgement of their 'citizenly' virtues and sacrifice. It could seem to them that there is much to be gained from being a nuisance, deviant or a problem for the state. Instead of having to struggle and scrimp for furniture and clothing, instead of living in dread of the next fuel or rates bill, instead of having to think of how to give the children a holiday or occupy them in the evening, it may be better to give up and call in the social services.

From working on a council estate in the north-east of England I came to realise just how widespread these feelings were towards clients, particularly from those whose circumstances were little different from those of the clients I was seeing. On one occasion we were confronted by a large group of youngsters outside the family service unit's house who had been sent down by their parents to take part in our 'exciting' intermediate treatment group. We just did not have room for them all, and it was clear that these excluded youngsters understood that the only way they were going to get the 'treats' going on inside was through being hassled by the law. On this estate, this was virtually the only way that young adolescents would be able to meet, sit round and drink cups of coffee with a degree of freedom!

From the outside, therefore, it can seem that some clients are on to a good thing. Non-clients often do not realise the ways in which clients are related to by the state, or the immense costs to their self-confidence and self-esteem that are exacted in return for certain short-term benefits. Rather, from the outside, it can seem that clients, many of whom function as a negative reference-point for their 'respectable' and struggling neighbours, are being rewarded for their deviancy. The world is thus turned upside down, with the consequence that 'respectable' neighbours become more embittered and angry about their client neighbours, and are equally hostile to the social workers involved.

CLIENTS AND STIGMA

The role of the mass media in shaping hostile opinions about sections of the client population should not be underestimated. While it would not be correct to argue that daily newspapers and television are the only creators of the stigma which is associated with problem families and juvenile offenders, they nevertheless fuel such attitudes and beliefs. In recent years there has been a spate of articles attacking social workers. Many of these have been concerned with developing the theme that social work in its supposed pandering of the deviant and nuisance poor typifies the decline of Britain, and is symptomatic of the collapse in moral standards which so many on the Right hold to be the main cause of the current recession and urban unrest. Paul Johnson typified this development when he wrote that 'social workers, vandalism and the flight of capital go together' (*Sunday Telegraph*, 9 July 1978; cited in Gilbert, 1979, p. 18). In these attacks on social work many writers have not hesitated to make vicious attacks on clients as one of their principal strategies for discrediting social workers. Thus in a *Daily Mail* article, Lynda Lee-Potter wrote that 'In almost every direction we've negated self-help and created a monster which supports the idle, feeds the feckless, acts as a nanny goat to layabouts,' (cited in Gilbert, 1979, p. 17). Statements such as these are not solely aimed at social workers. Rather, they are exploiting already strained relationships between clients and non-clients and providing ever more support for the cruel stereotypes of clients as parasites and scroungers who apparently will not work but will plunder the wealth they did not create.

Interestingly, *Social Work Today* recently gave space to one social worker who maintained that the tarnished image of the activity could be in part improved if social workers were seen to take a tougher line against certain 'undeserving' sections of the client population:

> There is, however, a hardy group of undeserving leeches who take all that is going and put nothing back. As a social worker and a ratepayer, I am beginning to resent the time and money wasted on a section that would possibly benefit more from being told: 'It's your problem, you deal with it.' A minor benefit from this approach would be an improved public image for us. If we were seen as supporting the deserving poor, rather than the feckless, we would have more likelihood of seeing something for our efforts, we would probably have more job satisfaction and we would at last be seen as doing something worthwhile.
>
> (Lamont, 1981, p. 17)

Although it is difficult to judge the extent of these views within social work, that such material appeared in *Social Work Today* does suggest the presence of a certain stream of thought within social work which does little to counteract the stigmatisation and isolation of some clients, and in many instances may exacerbate these problems.

The scapegoating of clients is difficult to fight. Nevertheless many social workers are acutely aware of this problem and attempt in their daily practice to prevent the labelling and stigmatising of clients. This low-level kind of work also involves many social workers attempting to defeat the many exaggerated myths that are circulated about clients. Ginsburg, for example, recalled a Glasgow study which demonstrated how the local press and corporation officials had amplified the stigma associated with problem estates. Yet these researches discovered that

> the violence, the criminality and depravity popularly associated with a slum estate was largely a myth, which was nevertheless so powerful and so insistently fostered that even the tenants of the estate believed in it and blamed their own neighbours for their plight.
>
> (Ginsburg, 1979, pp. 163—4)

The problem with such stigmatisation, whether it arises through the media or through the actions of state social policies, is not so much that it invents divisions and tensions where none existed previously, but that it distorts and deepens problems within the working class which have a material basis in many communities. Thus studies of working-class communities such as that by Coates and Silburn (1970) have observed that the conflict between 'problem families' and 'respectable' workers runs much deeper than any 'nuisance' the former are deemed to occasion. Instead, there is a complex of social relations ranging from sympathy and concern to outright hostility. Coates and Silburn, for example, noted that the problem families of St Annes

> certainly find formal association of any kind more difficult than other people, and they tend to live at some distance morally speaking from their neighbours. Reviled by many residents as the cause of all St Annes' difficulties, labelled by the authorities as multi-problem families, not only do they not accept any common identity, but will frequently express the most caustic opinions of one another.
>
> (Coates and Silburn, 1970, p. 154)

The physical and moral distance which so often separates clients from non-clients within the same community and which can lead to intra-class tension arises from a complex of interacting issues. Some of these are all too obvious, such as the policies pursued by some local housing authorities in isolating 'problem families' in physically distinct hard-to-let ghetto housing (Byrne, 1973). Then there are the wider problems of surviving poverty. For many clients the struggle to survive is time-consuming and exhausting, instanced by endless hours of bargain-hunting, managing with few or no domestic appliances, coping with inadequate methods for heating rooms and water, plus all the other struggles over clothing, housing, washing and food. For many of the dependent poor their diets deteriorate to such an extent that their health declines and lethargy and depression result (Newcastle Trades Council, 1980). Factors such as these greatly inhibit clients' possibilities for social interaction and their involvement in local tenant and community groups, and for many the sheer lack of cash closes off other points of contact such as the local pub, café or club. High transport costs have also heightened this isolation through reducing the mobility of those on low incomes or dependent on state benefits.

These are a few of the factors which can help to an understanding of the isolation of many clients which are of a very different order from those divisions and tensions which are either fuelled by the media or arise from the practice and operation of social welfare. The apparent individualism of many clients and their subsequent distancing from their neighbours and local communities is therefore not so much a symptom of their 'inadequate' personality but rather the consequences of survival in a largely hostile and uncaring society. For many clients, the sheer struggle to survive compels them to adopt the most individualistic and introverted strategies which are completely at odds with the traditions of collective action which have developed within the organised working class both in their communities and in their workplaces.

One consequence of this physical and moral separation of clients from non-client working people is that it is more difficult to oppose and eradicate the stereotyping of some clients as 'scroungers' and 'spongers'. Conversely, the dependent and residual poor are often influenced by the anti-union propaganda which accompanies many industrial disputes. For those on low and fixed state benefits the 'news' from the media that strike action and higher pay awards will inevitably mean higher prices can have a divisive impact. Conversely, it is also apparent that the government and employers are using the presence of a large reserve of labour to exert greater pressure on those in employment to limit their demands and to impose on the trade unions greater limitations. In these diverse ways class solidarity can be weakened.

Thus there are many factors and influences which inhibit the possibility of united class activity. The task facing many progressive welfare workers is that of identifying some of the divisive forces which separate so many of the client population from the rest of the working class and then devising strategies which could reverse the process. From the discussion so far it would seem that one fruitful area for exploration is that of seeking ways to encourage more contact between clients and non-clients that could include working to create the actual physical resources and meeting-places where such contact could develop. The problems confronting work of this kind should not be underestimated, for some of the intra-class divisions have long and bitter histories. Nevertheless, a recent publication of the Association of Community Workers, *Successes and Struggles on Council Estates* (1982), does support the importance and possibilities of such work, and in recounting a variety of tenant struggles to ensure the provision of estate facilities (youth clubs, play schools and groups) and the improvement of homes some important insights into how intra-class divisions can be eroded and united action secured are provided.

Initiatives such as these might also help to rekindle the bonds of comradeship which many working people perceive as having been weakened since the war. This theme, recounted in many of the recently published working-class accounts and histories, is particularly prominent in Jeremy Seabrook's powerful book *What Went Wrong?* (1978), and is exemplified by the following comments made by a shop steward in a Walsall foundry:

At work the attitude to anybody who is in hardship, whether it's accident, illness, old age, 'That's his fucking bad luck.' It never used to be like that. It used to be, 'Oh yes, what can we do to help, those things could happen to us any day.' Now it's fate. Bad luck. Old age is fate. It's mad. People's attitudes towards each other is ugly. People on the dole can't go into a pub for a drink because everyone will think they're scroungers. It's their own fault. It's no use using a balloon on a stick to fight capitalism, because they've got a bloody sword. There has been a softening up of working people as far as their own selves are concerned; a hardening up towards others.

(cited in Seabrook, 1978, p. 88)

There is a pressing need to pay attention to these views, to untangle their meaning and to discover the processes which have seemingly contaminated kinship and comradeliness in many communities, of which the scapegoating of client groups is just one example. Although there is more than sufficient evidence of generosity and comradeship continuing within working-class communities, the definite weakening of these humanitarian social relations must be recognised and more effort directed towards developing policies and practices which can rekindle those bonds and relationships which are so vital to the building up of a unified and radical working-class politics.

IDEALISM AND SOCIAL WORK

The manner in which social work has contributed to the fracturing of a more vital and united working-class response to the plight of the dependent and 'nuisance' poor is now explored, starting by focusing on the processes through which social work has contributed to the depoliticisation of clients' problems.

The depoliticisation of clients' problems, by which is meant the manner in which they are presented and understood in ways which deny or obscure their connection with the capitalist process, for example emphasising personal inadequacy, has been a central feature in the development and practice of social work. While this process is also evident within every state agency which has dealings with the working-class poor, it is particularly significant within the personal social services given that this part of the state apparatus deals almost exclusively with the residual and problem poor. Within the history of social work there exists a tradition which not only attempts to redefine the nature and causes of poverty and human brutalisation, but also to promote a view of clients not as casualties of a barbarous social system but more as a special and unique sub-species of the human race. Thus, whether they are described as 'abnormal', 'inadequate', 'disturbed', or 'immature', clients are presented as 'peculiar' human beings, whose peculiarity is the reason for their inability to live and function as 'normal'.

From this standpoint it is then possible to explain the material squalor and deprivations which characterise the circumstances of so many clients. Social work has never attempted to deny outright the material nature of client's problems, but rather locates it as a *symptom* of inadequacy. The following quotation from Octavia Hill is a particularly fine example of this logic, which although written nearly a century ago would undoubtedly find much support today:

> The people's houses are bad because they are badly built and arranged; they are tenfold worse because the tenants' habits and lives are what they are. Transplant them tomorrow to healthy and commodious houses and they would pollute and destroy them.

> (Hill, 1884, p. 10)

It is in part the manner in which social work has figured as a theory and practice of idealism — namely, the primacy accorded to personality in the determination of an individual's social condition — that permits it to be accused of depoliticising the problems of clients. It is not simply that a materialist stance has been neglected but that it has been rejected and fought against. Obviously, it is not the case that social work has refused to accept some materialist aspects as relevant.

Social work would have lost all of its credibility had it not acknowledged that squalid housing, for example, does have some effect on the people forced to live in it. What the main stream of social work has done for over one hundred years, however, is to insist upon the primacy of a particularly narrow form of idealism over materialism. It is thus still insisted that mind is more dominant than matter in the determination of the human condition. And it is still argued that with the 'right' set of moral and personal values it is possible for any human being to overcome the effects and consequences of crushing poverty. This emphasis on the primacy of the individual, and the concomitant belief in the power of character (of the 'right' sort), is precisely what underpins the reassertion of self-help and self-reliance which is so central to the Thatcher government's social policy strategy. As Margaret Thatcher argued in a letter to *The Times*:

> Millions on millions have worked out their salvation in every sense of the term from such beginnings [the slums], just as others have worked their opportunities. I look forward to the day when there will be no slums. But I believe that we shall achieve far more by helping people to help themselves than by trying to relieve them of their responsibilities and thereby of their own dignity and self respect.

> (*The Times*, 18 July 1977)

CORDON SANITAIRE

The process by which agencies such as social work have tended to remove clients from visibility and the public domain of political debate to the privatised world of the family and interpersonal dynamics has contributed to the obfuscation of an important source of anger and discontent within British society.

In this, social work undoubtedly gained strength and credibility from the fact that some clients do seem to behave irrationally, and many did not reap any obvious advantage from the post-war expansion of the social services or during periods of economic prosperity. Consequently, the notion that perhaps the causes of many client problems do in fact reside within the clients themselves has been able to take considerable root and gain influence. Similarly, with the popularisation of Freudian ideas in British culture as a whole, the specific ideas and theories of social work have not lacked a supporting milieu in which to flourish.

Whereas the organised labour movement was implacably opposed to such ideas during the latter part of the nineteenth century, when organisations such as the COS attempted to blame the poverty and destitution of even the 'respectable' working class on their morals, habits and life-styles, there has been no corresponding degree of outrage in the period since the Second World War when a similar message has been promoted with respect to large clusters of the new client population. This absence of criticism from organised labour cannot be solely attributed to the long-entrenched attitudes of disinterest and hosility towards the residual poor, though these traditions were not helpful in forging a radical response to some of the policies ennacted in the post-war period. Instead, the state's approach to the residual poor after 1945 was markedly different in its degree of liberality and concern. The tone and character of present-day state social work's individualistic approach has been significantly different from that articulated by the COS, especially with respect to the 'undeserving' poor. Thus to some degree the wedges which have been recently driven into the working class through the operation of social work ought in part to be considered as an aspect of the contradictory consequence of its individualising humanitarian ideology, which has had an effect in deflecting criticism.

This absence of sustained criticism also reflects a particular belief prevalent at least during the 1950s and early 1960s, i.e. that the twin forces of relatively full employment and an extended welfare state had combined to eradicate all the major material and structural causes of poverty, leaving behind in its wake only those whe were too inadequate to benefit from the progress made. This belief was well reflected in Crosland's *The Future of Socialism*:

If our present rate of economic growth continues, material

want and poverty and deprivation of essential goods will gradually cease to be a problem. We shall increasingly need to focus attention, not on universal categories, but on individual persons and families, not on the economic causes of distress, but on social and psychological causes ... We shall rely less on broad, sweeping measures of expenditure than on concentrated measures of aid to limited groups based on patient, empirical social research into the real nature of need. And the aid will often take the form, not of cash payments, nor even of material provision in kind, but of individual therapy, casework and preventive treatment. The tone of social expenditure may be set less by old age pensions, than by the Family Planning Association, child care committees, home visitors, almoners and mental health workers.

(Crosland, 1956, pp. 155—6)

Even though this complacency was not shared by all, even during the prosperous 1950s — least of all by many clients themselves — the attitudes on continuing poverty held by the middle-class intellectual leadership of the labour movement did undoubtedly enable the growth of a psychologistic approach to the problems of the poor. Moreover, it contributed to the depoliticising process of the labour movement as a whole by removing the ongoing problems of brutalisation and human destruction so evident among the client population from any direct relationship with the nature and character of capitalism. Indeed, it could almost be argued that the experiences and circumstances of clients in the immediate post-war period were as much an embarrassment to the reformist social democracy of the Labour party and the Trades Union Congress as they were to capital itself.

Consequently, many forces have combined together with the result of further marginalising clients and of drawing around that cluster of the population a *cordon sanitaire* which to all intents and purposes removes some of the most vivid examples of the failures of capitalism to satisfy even the basic human needs of all the population from the political arena to the privatised domain of personal pathology. This in turn reinforces the view that the solutions to problems of clients are to be sought in the efforts of welfare professionals rather than in fundamental and radical social change. As a result, one of the running sores of capitalism is politically sanitised, and clients — rather than becoming a source of outrage and a stimulus to militancy on account of their suffering and neglect — become at best objects of pity or at worst stigmatised outcasts who have only themselves to blame.

CONSTRUCTING AN ALTERNATIVE

The issues raised in this chapter point to a number of possibilities for those radicals and socialists employed in social work. One activity that immediately suggests itself is that of trying to break down the *cordon sanitaire* that has surrounded clients and to represent them as victims and evidence of a particularly immoral social system which demands revolutionary change. Given the leftward currents that are now re-emerging with greater strength among the rank and file of the labour movement, the time is opportune for more strenuous educational work by progressive social workers. In particular, there is a powerful case for social workers to challenge the idealist arguments embedded within social work and to develop an alternative which closely examines the mechanisms and processes of capitalism which undermine so many of the human qualities and possibilities of clients.

Possibly one of the most useful points for constructing such an argument is to be found in one of the classic accounts of working-class life, that written by Engels in the middle of the last century, *The Condition of the Working Class in England*. In many ways, this book puts some empirical flesh on the bare bones of Marx's statement regarding the manner in which capitalism is continually reproducing an impoverished population of surplus and residual labour: a *lumpenproletariat* (Marx, 1874, pp. 602–3). In doing so, Engels avoids the two extremes of romanticism and moralism. Very simply, when Engels came face to face with the shocking conditions and awful life-styles of some of the poor of Manchester, he took this as incontrovertible proof of the anti-human nature of capitalism. Unlike later generations of social reformers in the COS, for example, who were similarly shocked and appalled by the conditons of huge numbers of poor people, Engels was not concerned to perform theoretical acrobatics in order to deflect criticism from the obvious processes by which capitalism brutalised the poor: 'there is therefore no cause for surprise if the workers, treated as brutes, actually become such' (Engels, 1973, p. 137).

When the conditions and social relations which dominate the lives of so many clients are examined, it should similarly 'be no cause for surprise' that so many of them are 'damaged', that they sometimes do irrational things to one another and to themselves. Living on long-term social security benefits with no hope of any change; with no future and no chance of enjoying 'the good life' which is thrust forward in the soap operas on television; being on the receiving end of relationships with teachers, doctors, nurses, social security officers, housing managers, social workers, and so on, which undermines and carries explicit messages of failure and nuisance; living often in wretched housing conditions and on poor diets — all of these things, and more, can undermine the lives of clients.

It is not only social workers who often fail to address these kinds of issues, but many sections of the Left in this country have also failed to come to terms with the actual processes by which capitalism undermines and destroys vital human characteristics. Yet it is so often these dehumanising relations with state officials, combined with the acute problems of living in unremitting poverty, that produce the seemingly irrational behaviour and personality patterns that characterise some sections of the client population. There is much work to be done in order to understand the manner in which these processes and experiences decisively affect the well-being of people, and social workers are particularly well placed to contribute to this work of constructing a powerful alternative to the pervasive idealism which underpins the psychologistic explanations of so many social problems.

ANGER

According to Engels, one of the central day-by-day struggles affecting every proletarian is the struggle for humanity on the basis that a central tendency of capital is always to treat labour not as human but as a commodity: a 'thing'. As both he and Marx wrote time and time again, the struggle of workers to resist the dehumanising tendencies of capitalism is one of the most pervasive and continuous conflicts which goes on day in and day out and takes innumerable forms. Engels wrote:

> the relation of the manufacturer to his operatives has nothing human in it; it is purely economic . . . And if the operative will not be forced into this abstraction, if he insists that he is not Labour, but a man [*sic*], who possess among other things the attribute of labour force, if he takes it into his head that he need not allow himself to be sold and bought in the market as a commodity 'labour' the bourgeois reason comes to a standstill.

> (Engels, 1973, p. 276)

Ordinary life is continually confirming this struggle: from small acts of sabotage, to all-out strikes, from dress to music; from the demands for consultation on all matters affecting people's lives to outright civil disobedience, and in many other activities, individuals continually strive to assert their humanity in the face of industrial and state practices which attempt to deal with them as things, commodities, ciphers on a form. E. P. Thompson has suggested that 'resistance to capitalism's innate tendency to reduce all human relationships to economic definitions' has been, and remains, one of the great forces behind working-class movements:

> I have suggested that one way of reading the working class movement during the Industrial Revolution is as a movement of resistance to the annunciation of economic man . . . The more recent long struggle to attain humane welfare services is part of the same profoundly anti-capitalist impulse, even if advanced capitalism has exhibited a greater flexibility in assimilating its pressures.

> (Thompson, 1978, p. 84)

According to Engels, the struggle of working people against countless dehumanising processes was one of the most important ways in which they resisted being brutalised: 'This rage, this passion is rather proof that the workers feel the inhumanity of their position, that they refuse to be degraded to the level of brutes, and that they will one day free themselves from servitude to the bourgeoisie' (1973, p. 140). Yet, Engels noted, not all working people can sustain this anger against the system which impoverishes them and denies them the means for human existence. The pressures on those who are trying to survive in and around pauperism, the strain on personal relationships, and the tendency towards individualism in the face of such problems can all contribute to individuals and families giving up and succumbing to the forces of brutalisation. When this happens there would seem to be a significant shift in the direction of previous anger; instead of it being focused outwards, on to state agencies for example, it would seem to become introverted. As a consequence brutalisation could be understood as that process where anger is directed inwards leading to a wide variety of behaviours including drug and alcoholic abuse, glue-sniffing, domestic violence and suicide, all of which share the characteristic of self-abuse and destruction. Engels observed that these victims 'are tossed about by fate, lose their moral hold upon themselves as they have already lost their economic hold, live along from day to day, drink and fall into licentiousness, and . . . they are brutes' (1973, p. 140).

This passage from Engels is startlingly resonant with the descriptions of multi-problem families found in more recent social work texts (Stephens, 1945; Timms and Philp, 1957). But there the similarity ends, for where traditional social work has sought to explain such behaviour in terms of the 'moral fibre' of clients, Engels looked to the class structure of capitalism and identified the bourgeoisie themselves as being responsible for setting 'in motion the causes which give rise' to such brutalisation, self-destruction and despair. Similarly, Engels did not appear unduly surprised when some of those exposed to the greatest pressures on their ability to survive capitalism's barbaric thirst for profit succumbed and went under. In fact, Engels expressed surprise that so many were able to survive, and in the midst of squalor were able to sustain their humanity, and he marvelled over the evidence of comradeship, care and generosity that he discovered among the impoverished of Manchester. Social work, on the other hand, reverses this process. Little or no credit is accorded to the working-class poor who survive; their ability to withstand the pressures tends to be seen as 'normal' rather than distinctive and abnormal. These are the qualities reserved for the clients, the failures and the inadequates. As a consequence, clients are removed from any connection with capitalism and those able to survive its pressures. Social workers moreover are actively dissuaded from looking in these directions in order both to understand the problems of clients and to devise those strategies which might help them to offer valuable support and techniques for withstanding brutalisation.

There is much that can be learnt from Engels's work on poverty and brutalisation which can be of great value in the construction of socialist welfare work. For example, in contrast to those articles which have advised social workers how to deal with 'angry clients' (Waldron, 1958; Tilley, 1955) — 'by and large one tries to stir up their concern for themselves as individuals, their desire to live their lives a bit more adequately . . . to help them see that continually banging one's head against the wall of authority is a childish reaction, and that it is more adult to internalise discipline' (Tilley, 1955, p. 30) — ways should be explored of supporting and helping to sustain that anger in a manner that avoids the client being made vulnerable to aggressive state responses, and simultaneously protects them from despair and defeat. Engels has also provided some of the clues and insights required if an alternative view of clients is to be constructed so that they are no longer removed from their class context and made invisible. Thus instead of being a peculiar sub-species clients become seen as being at one end of a continuum of working-class experiences and reactions to surviving under capitalism which affect everyone, albeit to different degrees. Such as analysis has important political potential in breaking down some of the divisions which so weaken the possibilities of united class agitation.

However, there is much work to be done in developing these arguments, and a study written in the middle of the nineteenth century cannot present all the answers to present-day problems. But at least Engels's historical materialism provides some important signposts to this work, suggesting that progressive social workers should be working alongside clients and non-clients alike in order to identify those pressures which undermine essential human characteristics, perhaps rekindling a rage against those pressures, an essential precondition for socialist agitation.

WHERE SHOULD SOCIAL WORKERS WORK?

Ways in which the findings of such research can be communicated back to the working class and the labour movement also need to be considered. No amount of meticulous scholarship would be satisfactory if the results only circulated among the 'converted' and tiny numbers of socialist 'intellectuals'. For it to be successful, it not only has to consider the ways in which some clients are brutalised but also the reactions of the non-clients who can so often be moralistically condemning of their client neighbours.

Again, there are no easy answers to these issues. However, it is important to direct attention to this side of the task, and it is now possible to suggest tentatively a few sites which might be appropriate. There have been, for example, recent developments within a number of trades councils (Coventry, Liverpool . . . Trades Councils, 1980) and in the formation of unemployment centres and unions which suggest fruitful avenues for progressive social workers to explore. The publication by the Newcastle Centre for the Unemployed of *On the Stones* (1980) has as one of its clear aims the raising of consciousness among the labour movement about the manner in which the experience of unemployment destroys human lives. Work such as this which is clearly intended to fuel the anger of working people about the manner in which capitalism attempts to solve its problems at the expense of human feeling and life among huge sections of the working class (and is a much-needed response to the weight of the mass media which at times has deliberately misinformed and glided over the realities of unemployment) is entirely consistent with the tasks suggested in this chapter.

There are also now some progressive developments with respect to the mobilisation of the working-class old. As well as the important work of Task Force in this area (Buckingham *et al.*, 1979), there are organisations emerging such as the British Pensioners' Trade Union Action Committee (Phillipson, 1981) which are attempting to bring retired workers and the trade-union movement closer together. In terms of the long history whereby key structures of organised labour have excluded the majority of retired workers, these developments are of considerable significance in their attempt to bridge deep and historic divisions within the working class.

There have also been important initiatives taken by progressive social workers themselves. In Leeds, for example, a number of social workers formed the Leeds Social Work Action Group (SWAG) during the 1978—9 strike. This group was concerned to break the monopoly held by senior management over the plans and programmes of social services in Leeds. This group is now part of Leeds NALGO and, as some of the participants have written, 'this change [to NALGO] was an important one, since it put the social worker's plans at the core of the trade union movement. Organically SWAG had grown out of that movement; in the end it is hoped that variations on such [schemes] become the property and the policy of the working class movement' (Bolger *et al.*, 1981, p. 77). Certainly developments such as these can be repeated elsewhere and they are most necessary on two interrelated points. First, being based firmly within the trade-union movement they allow for a degree of protection to those social workers who are willing to use their on-the-job experiences in a wider radical context. Second, they allow for the possibility that the work of such groups becomes part of the discussions and debates taking place within the organised labour movement. Thus such groupings could provide excellent organisational settings in which to undertake the work of breaking down the many divisions which exist within the working class, and in restoring that stream of anger to the labour movement by unmasking the problems and circumstances of clients which have been so marginalised and sanitised in the past.

Finally mention should be made of the Labour party, in

the early 1980s passing through one of its most crucial periods of reappraisal. Virtually for the first time since the last war many Labour party activists have united to press for the most radical reappraisal of the party's politics, and after the intense disappointments of recent Labour administrations are pressing for the adoption of socialist policies and a more open and democratic party structure. In the debates and struggles surrounding the leadership, and in the formation of an Alternative Economic Strategy (AES), the rank and file of the Labour party are engaging in a most important political discussion. It is crucial that progressive social workers take part in these debates, not just as members of the Labour party, but as workers in the welfare state. Their work experiences can make an important contribution to these discussions and ensure that the debates concern not just economic policy but social welfare as well. The opportunity cannot be passed by of making sure that the circumstances of the working-class poor are publicised and considered. And social workers should take part in the formulations of radically different social welfare policies that are so necessary for the short-term benefit of clients and in the longer-term struggle for socialism.

DIVIDE AND RULE

Undoubtedly the 1980s recession with its massive levels of unemployment is a key factor in pushing these new initiatives. As more and more of the 'respectable' working class are plunged into unemployment and face the kinds of pressures and unsavoury social relationships with the state that have been the preserve of clients for so much of the post-war period, so the possibilities for real alliances between the client and non-client surplus population have been enhanced. But we are still only talking of possibilities that await political action. Previous periods of high unemployment and economic crisis both in the nineteenth and twentieth centuries remind us that the state does not stand idly by awaiting the formation of close alliances among the unemployed, and between the unemployed and the employed (Novak, 1978). Through the media, and through a whole complex of social policy initiatives, the state is continually attempting to divide the workless in order to prevent a unification of interests. Whether it is through pensions policies, retirement schemes, differential benefit provision, MSC policy, or redundancy schemes, the ways in which small differences are overlaid on the general condition of unemployment can be seen — differences which may be small but can have important consequences in setting the unemployed apart from one another. In late 1982 it was only too clear that the government was directly attempting to exacerbate age, racial and sexual differences as a means of fragmenting the workless.

The clients of social work are being directly embroiled in this attempt at divide and rule. As noted earlier in the book, there has been an attempt among some right-wing elements to present clients as one of the factors in the recession. There seems to be a direct implication that while many of the new unemployed are unfortunate victims of the recession, groups such as problem families are scroungers and spongers on the tottering welfare system. The alliance of possible interests is therefore being directly challenged by such interventions that reconnect directly with the past when such huge efforts were made to distinguish between the deserving and undeserving poor.

It is not surprising, therefore, that many client groups have experienced massive cutbacks in the *service* elements of state social work, which have included reductions in home-help provision, aids and adaptations, day centres, nurseries, and so on. Material aid under section 1 of the 1963 Children and Young Persons Act is also being more tightly regulated and new tougher provisions for juvenile offenders are being introduced. Similarly, there has been a massive reduction in the range of imaginative schemes — often funded under the urban aid programme — which developed in the most impoverished inner-city areas during the early 1970s. Adventure playgrounds, advice centres, drop-in clubs, estate coffee bars, community facilities, summer holiday play schemes and play buses are just a few of the casualties of government policy (Davies, 1980).

Toughening up the policies and services directed at the

client population has enormous implications in dividing the working-class poor. Along one dimension it allows for the assertion of difference between the client and non-client unemployed; on another level it can give the impression to the non-client poor that their plight is a cause of sadness to the state and that it does not hold them to be at fault for their condition, unlike some of those who who are clients. In so doing the policies and messages from the state clearly suggest that the non-clients should have no truck with their client neighbours, who are deemed quite a different problem. Similarly, there does seem to be attempts to make the social services departments like the old Poor Law Guardians. By moving increasingly towards tougher and more constraining interventions in the lives of clients it seems most probable that state social work will come to exercise a more explicit deterrent pressure on the working-class poor as a whole. Thus as state social work becomes evidently more unpleasant and humiliating for clients, so the pressure will increase for the dependent poor to seek out ways of surviving which avoid contact with state social work, and for many this will involve considerable hardship and suffering.

Thus, just as the possibilities are now more apparent for a closer alliance between sections of the client population and the organised labour movement, so too there are increasing countervailing measures at the level of the state which hinder such a union of forces. Such pressures indicate clearly the need for progressive workers within the welfare state to exploit their position in order to prevent greater divisions than are already apparent from occurring, and for work to be undertaken which clearly demonstrates the political nature of clients' problems, and their close relation with the working class as a whole.

In this work it is important to proceed on the basis of a continuum of class differences within the working class. As indicated earlier, some of the most damning critics of clients are those who are forced to neighbour with them and who are often little better placed materially than those who they sometimes accuse of being undeserving 'scroungers'. Very often the differences between a defined 'problem family' and one which somehow manages to survive, albeit hazardously, are very small. Of course, once the latter family suc-cumbs, then the differences widen as the downward spiral of debt and despair accelerates. Nevertheless, it is possible to demonstrate that so many of the problems confronting clients are those which are always present waiting to drag down and trap every individual who cannot withstand the pressures of capitalist society. If progressive social workers can begin to shed some light on these issues and feed them into the labour movement, then perhaps a real contribution can be made to the development of a socialist common sense which brings bourgeois reason to a standstill. It would be a common sense which fights against the irritation of unruly youngsters vandalising a community, or the family which allows their home to become even more dilapidated than it needs to be, and these 'usual' responses of blaming the victims would be replaced instead with a deep and seething anger against a society which created such problems in the first place. Without such a rage as a first condition then the chances for socialism remain remote, and many clients will remain outcasts in a social formation that produced them.

5

The Centrality of the Social Worker

INTRODUCTION

The extent to which social work as an activity operates either in the interests of the state in controlling nuisance and social expenditure, or in the interests of clients through providing welfare resources, depends largely (although not exclusively) on the social workers themselves. Indeed, as a form of state intervention in the lives of the working class, social work is distinguished by its highly intensive and personalised approach.

Social workers are almost unique among state workers in their degree of involvement with clients. For families on the non-accidental injury register, 'problem families', and juvenile delinquents, the social work task demands almost total immersion by the social worker in family relationships, emotions and feelings; virtually nothing that occurs in these clients' lives is regarded as insignificant or irrelevant. And in recent years, the widely publicised tragedies of child deaths in families supervised by social workers has intensified the pressure on social workers to know their clients 'inside out'.

This chapter will identify some of the primary tensions and contradictions which have beset social work and the state as a consequence of this intensely personalised welfare strategy. In particular, it will be argued that the nature of social work under capitalism imposes tremendous strains on social workers: pressures which can subvert even the most traditional and

conservative of caseworkers to the extent that they sometimes work in ways which are contrary to the state's interests,
often unintentionally and occasionally deliberately. These
dilemmas have been recognised by both employing authorities and the social work leadership, and have evoked a range
of countervailing measures of which professionalism has been
one of the most significant, though ironically, as discussed
later, this too has occasioned problems for contemporary
state social work.

THE IMPORTANCE OF THE SOCIAL WORKER

Social workers are at the very centre of this welfare strategy.
They are not simply the purveyors of a service but also very
often the service itself, for it is their capacity to form a
relationship with the client that is deemed to be at the very
heart of social work (Rodgers and Dixon, 1960, p. 160). This
centrality of the social worker rests essentially on the idealist
manner in which the majority of the problems of clients are
understood. Thus although there have been important
material changes in the composition of social work's client
population since the nineteenth century, contemporary
social work continues to insist upon the legitimacy of the
COS's perspective that the problem of clients lies primarily
in their morality and personality rather than in the social
structure. This decisive aspect of social work's prevailing
ideology was typified in the Society's monthly journal,
the *Charity Organisation Review*, when it was argued that

> There can be no doubt that the poverty of the working
> classes of England is due, not to their circumstances
> (which are more favourable than those of any other
> working population in Europe); but to their improvident
> habits and thriftlessness. If they are ever to be more
> prosperous it must be through self-denial, temperance
> and forethought.

(*Charity Organisation Review*, vol. 10, 1881, p. 50)

The congruence of this passage with Elizabeth Irvine's (later) account of problem families is clearly evident, as in both the focus is on the deficiencies of personality which are presented as the main causes of clients' problems:

> Foresight is lacking so that money which will be needed for necessities tomorrow is squandered today on luxuries, attractive rubbish or daydream stimulants such as the 'pictures'. There is in fact 'no sense of the value of money', no 'sense of time', and often 'no sense of property'; in fact, a failure to grasp three of the most basic elements in our culture.
>
> (Irvine, 1954, p. 26)

Or, as Bernard Bosanquet argued, 'social disorganisation is the outward and visible form of moral and intellectual disorganisation' (1901, p. 297).

The idealist underpinnings of social work cannot be stressed too highly. It is from this perspective that many of the distinctive features of social work have stemmed, as well as its claim that it can bring about a permanent and lasting solution to the problems of clients. It is a perspective which demands an individualised and personalised approach, for, it is argued, it is only in this way that the attitudes, values and morality of the client can be confronted and modified. Thus idealism has important implications for the style of social work practice and underlies the demand that social workers need to be gentle and thoughtful in their construction of a relationship with the client if the goal of changing inner values is to be successful. It is from such a standpoint that social work has also resisted demands for a more abrasive and authoritarian approach to clients on the grounds that clients will become defensive and/or hostile, thereby preventing the social worker access to their inner thoughts and feelings which are considered so important in the treatment relationship. Thus, as Octavia Hill argued:

> I am satisfied that, without strong personal influence, no radical cure of those fallen low can be effected ... if we are to place our people in permanently self-supporting positions it will depend on the various courses of action

suitable to various people and circumstances, the ground of which can be perceived only by sweet sympathy, and the power of human love.

(cited in Garrett, 1949, p. 220)

Many of those points raised by Hill remain pertinent to social work today. In rather more sober language, CCETSW reaffirmed the importance of personal influence as being the key to the possible success of social work:

The skills of social work lie in the use of self and of social relationships to help the identification and resolution of personal and social problems . . . The social worker is required to use his person as the main medium of intervention in whatever setting or from whatever organisational base he is operating.

(CCETSW, 1975, pp. 17, 35)

As these passages make clear, the success of the strategy rests on the ability of the social worker to influence clients' morality and general outlook on the world. To do this the social worker is expected to provide a model of upright citizenship for the clients to copy. In the words of one social worker, 'we are little bags of gold dust and as we go through the world we influence our clients through contact, a little bit of the dust rubbing off here and a little bit there' (Nokes, 1967, p. 34). According to Father Biestek, 'The importance of the client—worker relationship in social casework is almost impossible to exaggerate . . . it is the soul of casework . . . as the life-giving principle it vivifies every part of casework' (1954, p. 57). And in making the same point, McDougall and Cormack write that 'the degree of change likely to occur in a client's *attitude* is to a large extent dependent upon the sort of relationship existing between him and the caseworker' (1954, p. 50). This stress on the relationship and the ability of the social worker to effect change has also established another important feature of the social work strategy: namely, that the social worker must enjoy a degree of autonomy and discretion in the relationship. This is clearly crucial if the social worker is to 'get through' to the 'inner life' of the client and to adapt to the dynamism of the relationship. Consequently, the social worker needs to be trusted in practice, as it is deemed undesirable for the interaction between social worker and client to be regulated closely and directly by the employing authority, for to do so would jeopardise the therapeutic relationship.

THE PROBLEM OF CONTAMINATION

Despite a certain congruence between the desired methods of social work and its theoretical and philosophical foundations, actual practice has proved to be difficult. Many of these difficulties have focused on the social workers themselves and stem from their centrality within this welfare strategy — their capacity to act as virtuous and trusted representatives of the state providing models of super-citizenship with which to inspire clients back to 'normality'. One of the principal areas of difficulty has been the demand that social workers, apart from being upstanding representatives of prevailing social attitudes and relations, are also expected to be concerned and friendly in their approach to clients. Thus, unlike many of those in the dominant class, social workers are not expected to hold aggressive and stigmatising attitudes with respect to the dependent and residual poor. Rather, as Younghusband wrote, social workers need to be tolerant, empathic and have the 'ability to get on with all sorts of people' (1947, p. 3), which was echoed by the Curtis Committee's recommendation that the new posts of children officers to be established under the 1948 Children's Act should be given to those social workers who are 'genial and friendly in manner and able to set both adults and children at their ease' (1946, p. 148).

It is this demand and expectation that social workers should ascribe to such liberal and humanitarian values and demonstrate a genuine concern for the welfare of the poor that has occasioned some of the persistent difficulties for social work. These, quite simply stated, relate to the difficulties of controlling and containing these qualities within the narrow parameters of idealistic social work. Since the time of the COS social work leaders have been alarmed to observe the reactions of some of their workers once plunged into the lives and communities of clients who, it would seem, have become victims of their emotions and are so disturbed by their experiences that they jettison the preferred methods of social work and 'go native', taking the side of the clients. This problem for established social work was particularly well expressed by Katherine Kendall, an influential American social work writer, when she wrote that

> vigorous concern with social problems and effective methods of dealing with them are precisely what we want [but the] dream waxes as we listen to idealistic young social workers proclaim their solidarity with the masses of people everywhere who have been shut out from a decent existence. The nightmare descends as we hear them reject the painfully acquired core of knowledge of man and society which could help them demonstrate a competence compounded of more than love, commitment and their own limited experience.

(Kendall, 1972, p. 7)

The problems of social worker 'contamination' and the manner in which social workers have become less than committed to the idealist perspectives of established social work have taken a wide variety of forms which have changed over time (see also Chapter 6 and 7). It has included, for example, low-level strategies of professional deviance whereby social workers have turned a 'blind eye' to clients manipulating the social security system; being less rigorous than many social work managers would like in the use of material aid, especially under section 1 of the 1963 Children and Young Persons Act; and preparing social enquiry reports in juvenile court proceedings which protect some youngsters from the more punitive aspects of the legal system (Pearson, 1975, p. 136). More recently there have also been open and public demonstrations of social workers taking the side of clients, one of the most notable being the stand taken by some social workers in the London Borough of Islington, in the early 1970s who stood alongside squatters behind the barricades constructed to prevent eviction.

Thus one of the prevailing and central preoccupations of social work throughout its development has been the problem of how to prevent social workers from being deflected and subverted from the occupation's 'divine ideals', of how to sustain social workers' commitment to its idealist perspectives, and to ensure that social workers bear the mantle of super-citizens so that they can achieve their desired remoralising objectives. This concern has been at the forefront of social work's long struggle to establish a 'professional' identity, and although this thirst for professional recognition has always been overlaid with wider ambitions to become an accepted and discrete part of the state's welfare system, with corresponding power, an equally important but neglected theme has been its internal preoccupation with moulding the strengths and aptitudes of social workers themselves. It is this 'internal' theme that has been particularly influential in shaping the character of social work professionalism and largely responsible for the pace of its development.

THE COS: THE ORIGINS OF SOCIAL WORK PROFESSIONALISM

Some of the first claims regarding social work's professional stature were made by the Charity Organisation Society. Indeed, one of the principal objectives of the COS's founding members was to transform philanthropy from an unskilled 'duty' of the rich to an expert and professional activity undertaken only by those who were prepared by social theory and trained in the appropriate methods. According to the Society's secretary:

> Doctors have to be educated methodically, registered and certificated. Charity is the work of the social physician. It is to the interests of the community that it should not be entrusted to novices or to dilettanti, or to quacks.

> (Loch, 1906, p. xix)

This was no simple demand for status but part of what the COS regarded as being among its principal objectives, namely to modernise charity and bring it into line with the prevailing needs of an advanced and, by the end of the nineteenth century, largely urban-based capitalist society. For the COS this need arose because of the widespread, and in its eyes ill-considered, philanthropy of the wealthy who were seeking to defuse the social and class tensions of the period through handing out small amounts of material aid. This 'feudal' approach to philanthropy, as the COS described it, had to be curtailed, for according to the Society's theorists and propagandists not only was this material assistance too small and too haphazard in its distribution to work effectively as a bribe for social tranquillity, but it was having the most deleterious effect on the already fragile morality of the poor.

Charles Loch well recognised the hardship of wage labour, particularly for the unskilled working class, and understood that the easy availability of doles and alms offered the workers a less arduous alternative means of survival independent of the labour market. Thus he insisted that his own class which engaged in such activity had to recognise that the giving of material aid to the destitute was not only ineffective (if the goal of such largesse were social tranquillity) but also demoralising to workers as a whole, for 'what a man sees done for his neighbour, he thinks he is entitled to himself, and he yields to self-indulgence, well aware that there is charity in the background. There is abundant evidence in proof of this' (Loch, 1906, pp. l–li). And if one is to believe the evidence presented by Helen Bosanquet, then the effect of material philanthropy on labour discipline during the last quarter of the nineteenth century was dramatic: 'tens of thousands of mendicants march forth every morning not to work or to seek work — but to beg; not to contribute by their industry, but to prey upon those who do' (1914, p. 4).

This example of intra-class conflict from the early days of modern social work is given to illuminate an important theme in the character of social work's professionalism and the manner in which it has been developed to sustain the 'faith' and perspectives of social workers. For in the struggle to outlaw almsgiving — and the COS was strongly resisted by those among the bourgeoisie who felt that the COS's idealist casework approach was hard-hearted and 'unChristian' (Yeo, 1973) – the Charity Organisation Society, with considerable success and support, used the argument that philanthropy should no longer be regarded as a conscience-salving pastime of the rich but a skilled activity which, as Loch asserted, required preparation and training. In making this argument COS members constantly drew attention to the 'evils' which awaited the soft-hearted and sentimental and pressed the need for training and the application of 'scientific' principles. Urwick, who for a time was director of the COS's School of Sociology which launched the first formal social work education programme in Britain in 1903, typified these arguments: 'the impulse to do good, may if untrained, lead straight to evil doing . . . the good heart unschooled by the good head will probably fall into dangerous paths – in a word . . . training is an essential for social service as for other kinds of service' (1904, p. 180).

THE STRUGGLE FOR CLOSURE

Between 1869 and the outbreak of war in 1914 the COS made substantial progress in its struggle to transform philanthropy, and developed many of the features of an aspiring profession, among the most obvious being the formal social work courses that were established in their School of Sociology (see Jones, 1976). But these courses were only the tip of an extraordinarily broad and informal education and training system which the COS had developed in the last two decades of the nineteenth century. Prominent in this informal network was the Society's monthly journal which contained numerous articles on how to undertake 'good' casework and in particular articles which established and legitimised the idealist underpinnings of its strategy.

The intent behind such developments were principally twofold. The most obvious was the COS's concern to train and educate its own workers. The second, and more neglected aspect, was to establish a new status for charitable work and, by stressing the need for education, to institute closer control over charity and close off this area of activity from uninformed intrusion. Max Weber was particularly astute in drawing attention to the manner in which such groups use education as a means of 'closure' and of consolidating their control:

> When we hear from all sides the demand for the introduction of regular curricula and special examinations, the reasons behind it is, of course, not a suddenly awakened 'thirst for education' but the desire for restricting the supply of these positions and their monopolisation by owners of educational certificates.
>
> (Weber, 1948, p. 241)

The concept of *closure* is particularly useful for illuminating the history of social work professionalism and the long-standing concern to protect social workers from possible contamination. In the case of the COS the early impetus towards professionalism was in no small part due to its drive to modernise philanthropy and to keep out those 'Lady Bountifuls' who 'lacked any understanding of labour questions or feeling for citizenship' and who had 'a patronising attitude towards the manual working class, with pity and regret for their ignorance, all these are pitfalls for the un-occupied, untrained, well-to-do women of today' (Hutchins, 1913, p. 51). Increasingly, however, social work has used its professional closure techniques as a means of controlling access to the occupation and as a way of keeping out those ideas and theories that challenge its idealist perspectives on the problems of clients and poverty in general.

The concern with access has been and remains a particularly important feature of social work professionalism. Thus from the time of the COS there has been a prevailing interest in the personal qualities of intending social workers and a corresponding assertion that social work requires particular qualities from its practitioners. In these arguments social work leaders have been especially anxious to squash the idea that anyone with a compassionate disposition can do social work. This profane image of social work — 'the idea that social casework consists in making arrangements and being a friend' (Younghusband, 1956, p. 242) — has irritated the social work leadership over the years, for it clearly weakens their arguments concerning the professional stature of the work. That is not to say, however, that social work disregards the value of certain personal qualities, far from it. The contention is that personal qualities of compassion and concern are needed but that alone they are insufficient, as was made clear in the 1967 Report of the Council for Training in Social Work:

> Experience over the years has taught us that many people, but not all, have the human resources of concern, tact, perception and common sense so necessary to good social work ... Whilst right attitudes are essential, these alone are not enough to help people whose problems are often complex and whose circumstances are subject to pressures, both internal and external, which require knowledge and understanding.
>
> (CTSW, 1967, p. 2)

Underlying these claims that 'it is not the sole condition of effectual work to have the kindly or even controlled religious mind, [it] must be supplemented by some equipment in the special knowledge, in the art of the visitor' (Loch, 1923, p. 32) is the recognition of the contaminating qualities of the clients themselves. The social work leadership has never underestimated the difficulties of doing social work, and especially of plunging liberal and compassionate middle-class individuals into the lives and homes of some of the most improverished sections of the population. The pressure on the emotions of social workers can be considerable, and social work theorists have recognised that there is a great danger of social workers becoming 'victim of their senses'. Thus the valued qualities of gentleness and kindliness on their own can lead the social worker to take uncritically the side of the client and so determine their interventions by the immediate evidence of material deprivation.

What is at issue here is the difficulty of implementing an idealist welfare strategy in situations where there is abundant evidence of material problems. The idealist stance of social work demands that welfare workers should take one step back from the immediate sensations of poverty and squalor and view the material deficiencies as a symptom of inadequate morality or, in the more modern parlance of social work, as a sign of an inadequate personality. Thus without some coherent theoretical preparation that allows social workers to offset the emotional impact of poverty, the danger lurks that they may side with clients' materialist interpretation of their problems and so rule out any possibility of engaging in the necessary remoralising work which social work theory demands. It is little wonder, therefore, that so much of the social work literature focuses on the manipulative qualities of clients, highlighting the manner in which clients can exploit the sympathies of the unguarded social worker. However, the writers of such texts do not situate their arguments in the context of the political clash of ideologies — of working-class materialism confronting bourgeois idealism — but in the more anodyne language of applied social science such as transference and counter-transference, presenting problem, client manipulation, which sound respectable and authoritative.

PROFESSIONAL SELECTION: PROCEDURES AND CONCERNS

The concern with ensuring the strength of social workers to resist such contamination is highlighted most clearly in the development of formal social work education. The next chapter briefly examines some of the issues raised by the content and structures of professional courses, but here the focus is on the attention given to selection procedures, for these are regarded by the profession as profoundly important, as witnessed by an American writer's comment that

One of the most crucial responsibilities of schools of social work is the adequate selection of qualified candidates for professional education. To achieve the major objectives of social work, it is necessary to select people who are best suited to perform professional roles.

(Patel, 1972, p. 128)

This assessment of the importance of selection was reinforced by Heraud's doctoral research on professionalisation in social work in which he argued that

the selection process probably represents the key structural variable in social work education. It is vital because it acts as a filter by which those who are seen to be 'fit' to be professionally certified are separated from those who, in various ways, are not. The process selects out those who are already minimally fit for practice in what appears to be a rigorous manner and therefore makes the task of socialisation during training easier.

(Heraud, 1972, p. 349)

Although the proportion of trained social workers has now risen considerably in the last decade the occupation has had to endure a long period in which only a minority of social workers were professionally certificated. Social work adjusted to this situation by regarding its professionally qualified workers as the leading cadre who would embody the values and techniques of social work and be capable of supervising and guiding those who had not undergone training. Thus it was particularly important that those selected for training should have the strongest 'identification with the ideals and objectives of his profession as well as with the group he serves. He must have an unwavering conviction as to the worth of the ends of his work' (Towle, 1954, p. vi). In other words, the social worker must be a supercitizen: a person of the 'highest' moral calibre, well able personally to represent the state to its clients. In terms of selection, therefore, those entrusted to act as the guardians of the profession were charged with choosing those who demonstrated the highest moral standard. As one COS tutor wrote: 'The best [social] workers must be the best human beings, those whose conduct of their own lives is most nearly what we wish the conduct of all lives to be' (Gow, 1900, p. 110). This sentiment has been echoed more recently by Gardiner and Judd, who maintained that 'The best social worker is the one whose own good citizenship is at the same time rational and infectious' (1959, p. 195). In other words, intending professionals had to demonstrate the virtues and character of model citizens who 'must be in accord with the social system they are helping to operate in dealing with its misfits . . . if this were not so we should probably not be caseworkers' (Corner, 1959, p. 21), or as Heywood has argued:

> because social workers have to stand for social values and require high ethical standards . . . we require some assurance that certain standards of behaviour and ideals have been laid down and securely founded in early life, and have been again thought out and incorporated by the candidate himself in adolescence.
>
> (Heywood, 1964, p. 9)

One could go on and give endless examples of social work tutors outlining the qualities they expect of prospective professional social workers. What is noteworthy, however, is not that such virtues should be highly regarded, after all social workers are supposed to provide the inspiring models of citizenship for their clients to copy, but that these qualities should be present *prior* to the professional training. Thus, unlike some socialist critics of social work who have attributed tremendous powers to social work courses successfully to socialise social workers into its idealist world-view (e.g. Coates and Silburn, 1970, pp. 16–17; Sinfield, 1974, p. 72), a closer examination of social work education demonstrates that a predisposition to this world-view is expected among candidates almost as a condition of acceptance to the course, and the course itself less ambitiously concerns itself with enhancing and fortifying that predisposition.

This determination with respect to selection – and in the late 1940s and early 1950s it was common for many applicants to undergo extensive interviews with psychiatrists (Younghusband, 1951) during the selection process – reflects social work's recognition of the difficulty of maintaining an idealist theory and practice when confronted with clients who are self-evidently materially deprived and located in the largely invisible bottom end of a grossly unequal social system. There is, however, no pretence that professional training and education alone can secure the commitment of the neophyte professional. For the social work enterprise there has to be evidence of an already firm predisposition to its goals, and in particular some indication that the candidates are not likely to abandon this position once they are immersed in practice.

SCIENTISATION

What professional education can do, however, is to strengthen and develop that predisposition. The ways in which this is done are numerous but it is possible to identify an overriding theme of the scientisation of morality which is evident throughout many parts of the social work curriculum. Very baldly stated, this theme refers to the way in which social work writers, aided and supported in many instances by a wide range of social sciences, have attempted to transform and disguise social work's class-based morality into a 'science' with its accompanying status of neutrality, authority and righteousness.

Although there have been many social work theorists who have shown a genuine interest in the capacity of the social sciences to shed further insights into the nature of social behaviour and problems, the prevailing trend in the history of social work's knowledge base has tended to be less serious and more pragmatic and eclectic. This trend is evident in the manner in which many social work writers have adopted a 'looting' approach to the social sciences, extracting and using only those elements which support and justify their approach and perspective and discarding those parts which challenge or contradict them. In this 'looting' approach social work writers have been particularly concerned with drawing into social work theory the language and concepts of science as a means of enhancing its status. There is considerable

evidence throughout the history of social work that demonstrates this preoccupation with image-enhancing procedures;
among the latest examples there are the emergence of higher
degrees, M.A.s or M.Sc.s, instead of the ordinary diploma.
Although some of the image-creation techniques do attract
ridicule, such as describing walking-sticks as 'mobility aids',
there is a serious intent behind many of the name changes.
This intent is concerned to establish through the kudos of
science, certification and other professional rituals a more
convincing legitimation of social work's essentially moralistic
perspectives on the problems of clients.

In part social work has engaged in this process in order to
shed its public image of 'do-gooding condescension' which
was clearly crucial if it were to gain support from the state,
especially in more recent years. But equally important, social
work has had to establish its scientific credentials in order to
convince the liberal middle classes who form the majority of
those employed as social workers that their intervention in
the lives of the working-class poor was distinctly different
from that of their Victorian predecessors. Thus whereas it
was possible to encourage and mobilise large numbers of the
bourgeoisie and middle class, in the mid-nineteenth century
to undertake charitable work with the urban poor on the
grounds that such people were barbarians awaiting and
needing moral guidance if they were ever to be civilised
(Taylor, 1972), such a clarion call in present-day society
might attract some support but not, one would suspect,
from the liberal middle-class people who enter social work.

Even towards the end of the nineteenth century the COS
was forced to drop its 'deserving/undeserving' classification
of destitute people and replace it with a new classification
of 'helpable/unhelpable' because it was accused of narrow
class-based moralism. Thus we find Urwick, the director
of the Society's School of Sociology, reflecting in 1904 on
the need to change the language of social work's 'essential
truths' because the students were unhappy with their evident
class pedigree:

> The terms in which our truths are expressed often belong
> to a past age; have we not all been at times uneasily

conscious that the mere appeal to fundamental principles of self-help, independence, thrift and the like, has lost much of its force, and that these principles must be recast, brought into new connections with current ideas and ways of thinking, clothed in new language? For it is unquestionably true that the new generation is receptive enough, but as always demands a new preparation of its food.

(Urwick, 1904, p. 182)

Many social work writers and teachers seem to have followed Urwick's advice over the past thirty years and have clothed their 'essential truths' in a new language. Younghusband, for example, has provided a clear example of the manner in which social work has been alert to the respectability that the language of science can confer:

[social science and research] make it respectable to talk about 'factors in social pathology' instead of the un-deserving poor; 'community stimulation' instead of getting lonely people along to the Settlement social; 'providing positive incentives to socially acceptable behaviour' instead of helping with the Brownie Pack; 'psychopathic personali-ties' instead of hopeless scroungers; 'rehabilitating the socially maladjusted instead of trying to reform anyone or anything. The essential rose remains unchanged by this change in names but, if anyone is helped thereby to see more clearly, to think more deeply, to diagnose more truly, and to treat more effectively, then this change and all others that succeed it are all to the good.

(Younghusband, 1947, pp. 61–2)

Yet again, while such image-creating practices are clearly useful in social work's attempt to gain recognition as a pro-fessional activity and are functional to its closure concerns, it is our contention that their primary target has been the social workers themselves: to sustain their confidence and to create and support a self-image of neutral expertise as a legit-imation of their personalised penetration in the lives of clients and to offset those criticisms which have accused social workers as being little more than middle-class moral entrepreneurs (Smith, 1957, p. 2). This argument is supported by a group of students who remarked:

> We decided that we undertook the course to become trained social workers ... We noted the importance of professional status as indicating a body of knowledge and degree of skill, as opposed to mere do-goodery, and as a defence of one's position.

> (cited in Anon., 1968, appendix B)

COUNTERVAILING IDEOLOGIES

Alongside the pressures arising from the direct experience of practice social work has also had to contend with a wide range of influences from outside its immediate domain which have contributed to a weakening of social workers' resolve and commitment. Despite the support social work ideology gains from ruling-class ideas in general, it is by no means the only explanation available which accounts for the persistence and character of the residual poor in capitalist societies. Marxist theory contains a very different explanation of the same phenomenon, and is one which turns mainstream social work theory on its head in its emphasis on the *material* realities of capitalism and its effects on human life. Marxism has been one of a number of radicalising influences which have had influence in social work during the past decade.

Perhaps more important than Marxism, however, has been the influence of feminism and the women's movement. With its critique of the family and the manner in which women are exploited and oppressed within it, feminist ideology directly confronts many of the central themes of mainstream social work culture. Similarly, feminism has sharpened the awareness of the many women who work as social workers and alerted them to the ways in which they are oppressed and disadvantaged as women workers. For example, despite the fact that the majority of social workers employed are women, the upper-management echelons of the occupation have been dominated by men. In the probation service, for instance, Brown and Foren note 'that it is clear that the woman officer is less likely to be promoted than the male and those that achieve senior ranks are, on average, better qualified, both educationally and professionally than the men' (1970, p. 8). Similarly, Walton has observed that since 1945 the number of women holding senior management positions has steadily declined as the personal social services have expanded despite the fact that just over half of social services personnel were women (1975, p. 236). Thus in April 1971, following Seebohm reorganisation, of the 160 new social services directors appointed, only fourteen were women.

The growing influence of feminism has not only affected the internal politics of social services departments but also the actual practice of social work. More and more women social workers are exploiting their limited freedom in their relationships with clients, not as a means of remoralising working-class mothers so that they can efficiently socialise their children in accordance with dominant values, but rather as a means of support and feminist consciousness-raising.

Thus there are now many social workers employed who would question the legitimacy of persuading a woman to remain within a family where the husband dominates and physically intimidates the wife. And whether in one-parent family groups or in family casework relationships, feminist politics and ideas are now being used by some social workers in a manner which clearly subverts the state's vision and intention for social work as a method of reinforcing a specifically bourgeois family type in which women are expected to be content with their unpaid role as the physical and moral reproducers and maintainers of labour.

CONCLUSION

Alongside all the other contradictions which make social work such a problematic activity for the state — its 'softly-softly' style, its holism and potential liberality — there now must be added the problem of the social workers themselves.

Moreover, recognition of this feature not only affords a more precise understanding of the dynamic character of social work but also bolsters belief in the potential of social workers to act in ways that favour the clients and to contribute valuably to the struggle for a radical change in society.

6

Social Work Education: Sustaining the Faith

INTRODUCTION

The national community as a whole now commands the services of thousands, indeed millions of other individuals, who are not civil servants in the strictest sense: policemen, firemen, postmen, the employees of the National Health Service (including a high proportion of the medical profession), the employees of local government (including the bulk of the teaching profession), and so forth. Effective government requires the obedience and the co-operation of all of these, and the only phrase that seems to meet the need is 'servants of the State'.

(Beloff, 1979, p. 7)

Even if one takes a most cursory overview of the recent history of social work, one feature that stands out is the extent to which increasing controls have been introduced for governing the activities and work of social workers. The range of measures has been wide and varied, and has included large-scale changes in the organisation of social services departments, with their expanded bureaucratic management hierarchies, more direct supervision over the social worker, and an expanded array of work processes which attempt to direct and regulate the social worker's contact with clients. These changes are explored in detail in Chapter 7; this chapter examines some of the key factors which have given rise to them.

CONTAMINATION

The social work leadership has always been concerned about the 'strength' of social workers in maintaining their idealist perspective on social problems when they are on their own in working-class communities. For the COS, one of its main concerns about its workers was their tendency to become over-involved in the client's problems, or, in the words of Bernard Bosanquet, their tendency to become 'victims of their senses' so 'indulging themselves' by 'being carried away by the first impression of unreasoned pity' (1893, p. 226). Here Bosanquet is referring to the apparent manner in which some COS visitors found it very difficult to withhold material aid from claimants in order to relieve their immediate destitution. In the first instance, all that COS visitors were supposed to do was to undertake a thorough enquiry into the claimant's life — asking landlords, neighbours, local shopkeepers, relatives, the parish priest, etc., about the claimant's character and general moral state — and visiting the home to assess cleanliness and order. They were then to report back to the local COS district committee with their assessment and, with the committee, determine whether the claimant was 'curable', and if so what treatment strategy was required.

This committee system instituted by the COS was one of its primary mechanisms for regulating the work of its charity visitors. In terms of decision-making, it was the district committee that was sovereign, and it was here that the plans for the charity worker's interventions were made. Consequently from the very beginning of modern casework practice constraints were placed on the autonomy of the individual social worker. Under the COS system the charity worker was seen as being very much the instrument of the district committee, and the individual would operationalise its plan of intervention. In many ways this form of organisation closely resembles modern forms of supervision, in particular the practice of contemporary case conferences, whereby it is the case conference which decides upon the general parameters of the case in question and sets out the guidelines for the social worker to follow.

However, as the nineteenth century progressed, the COS began to be confronted increasingly by challenges to their workers' commitment other than that of over-emotional involvement. For as class conflict deepened during the 1880s with increasing poverty, destitution and unemployment, and the accompanying politicisation of the working class and labour movement, the reform intelligentsia among the bourgeoisie began to split over the best means for restoring social order. Although there was a wide range of fractions within the reform intelligentsia, there were two main positions. One camp, centred largely upon the Charity Organisation Society, maintained that the best and most appropriate strategy for long-term social tranquillity was the policy of a two-tiered system of relief: one tier being the Poor Law which should deal with the hard-core undeserving poor, and the other being voluntary casework as established by the COS which would deal with the deserving and genuine poor and unemployed (Jones, 1978, ch. 3). Its opponents, of a Fabian perspective, argued that, given the size of the problems, voluntary welfare was altogether inadequate for the task and that the solution rested in the state taking a more active and interventionist role in social policy (Aldern, 1905; Townshend, 1911).

As Harris (1972) and Stedman Jones (1971) have illustrated, the debate within the reform bourgeoisie over this period was intense. Both sides engaged in a considerable propaganda campaign — the COS, for example, appointed a propaganda officer whose sole task was to scan newspapers and to reply to opponents and critics of the Society — in order to influence public opinion and government policies. But the COS was also confronted with the evident danger that its own workers would possibly defect to the other side. From the beginning the COS was aware that its charity workers were under immense strain trying to maintain their detailed, time-consuming and invidualised approach when all around them they saw collective poverty and misery. As Shairp wrote in his *Hints for Visitors*, it was essential that charity visitors should

not be appalled by the difficulty of serving. Above all we

must not be appalled by the great mass of poverty and trouble which we believe to exist, and which is so often set before us in the columns of the newspapers with vivid details and heart-rending appeals to assist thousands of starving. We need not exaggerate. It is quite enough for us to believe that we can, each of us, find one or two whom we may befriend.

(Shairp, 1910, p. 13)

The main source of contamination for the COS was the evident attraction of large-scale social reform sponsored by the state which promised more dramatic improvement than did casework. By 1916 the COS was having considerable difficulty in attracting workers following the welfare measures enacted by the Liberals between 1906 and 1912. Bernard Bosanquet noted in that year:

I suspect that young workers, otherwise desirous to help us and throw in their lot with us, are apt to be put off by a certain slur which may be cast on our work, and I should like to say a word about it, because I am prepared to fight this point to the death. I suspect that our work and methods are often compared unfavourably with ideas which favour more complete social reconstruction. Our work may be held 'second best', a palliative, not the real thing, not 'drastic' — an attractive word . . . the people are naturally attracted by what seems to promise more brilliant and universal results — social reconstruction of one kind or another. To work for this seems like working for a new heaven and a new earth, whilst we seem content with the old ones.

(Bosanquet, 1916, pp. 130–1)

In order to prevent such a demoralisation among its own ranks, the COS engaged in an active and imaginative educational programme, especially between 1895 and 1912, which it directed principally at its own workers and recruits. A common thread of that programme was the theme that the state was totally incapable of identifying and providing the personalised remoralisation which the 'deserving' working-class poor were deemed to require, and, moreover, that it was potentially more dangerous than indiscriminate almsgiving in that it would not only weaken self-help and self-reliance among the working class, but that it would also create expectations among the poor which could not be fulfilled within the existing social framework. Thus writing in the *Charity Organisation Review* Loch asserted that

> To shift the responsibility of maintenance from the Individual to the State is to sterilise the productive power of the community as a whole . . . It is also to demoralise the individual. No social system of rewards and punishments . . . will be a substitute for the influence of the social law by which energy, honesty and ability have their own reward, and failure in these things carries with it its own penalty. If our natural morality were a mere artificial system, such methods might avail. But it is of the very stuff of which we ourselves are made; and these artifices of legislation will but touch the merest surface of our social life.

(Charity Organisation Review, April 1895)

But as the divisions deepened within the reform intelligentisia, and as the 'Fabian side' clearly gained in influence towards the end of the nineteenth century, so the COS stepped up its educational programme. A new training sub-committee was established by the Society in 1897 and its first report warned the policy-making council that many of its district committee members showed 'a want of grasp of the principles for which the Society exists, and a want of enthusiasm for their fulfilment' (Training Committee, 1898, p. 130). It was in order to counteract these deficiencies and to strengthen the resolve of its charity workers that the COS began to develop formal social work education courses, and in 1902 established its School of Sociology in London (Jones, 1976). In setting up this formal institution the COS was explicitly meeting the challenge of the Fabian Society, which a few years earlier was largely responsible for inspiring the formation of the London School of Economics. Thus the conflict between the two main perspectives on social reform was now concretely epitomised by the two rival schools, both of which were concerned with turning out a cadre of experts fully committed to their respective ideologies and methods (Jones, 1978, ch. 8).

As with present-day social work courses, one of the main purposes of the School of Sociology was to socialise the students into the 'divine ideals' of social work. That socialisation should be such a preoccupying theme of social work education is indicative of the problem of 'securing' individual social workers in such a way as to protect them from the contamination of other sources and ideas. This core objective of social work education was well stated by Marshall, who wrote that the 'prime aim' of social work courses was

> to satisfy the personal needs of social workers themselves, to prevent internal mental conflicts, and to answer questions which they are bound to ask and must be enabled to answer if they are to give themselves whole-heartedly to their work inspired by a sense of purpose. In this connection I should like to refer once more to McIver's book [*Contribution of Sociology to Social Work*]. He points out the limitations of social work; the services offered are often only palliatives, leaving root causes unaffected. It may even be that they perpetuate the causes by making the effects more tolerable. Yet the social worker is moved by an emotional desire to help in the creation of a better world. How can this urge be reconciled with the limitations of the daily task? And he answers: 'The social worker must in short be socially educated, must acquire as a student of economics and sociology, a background of intellectual convictions. So fortified, he or she can advocate further goals while still doing a day's work ... The social worker who has no background of social philosophy is at the mercy of a thousand discouragements.'

(in Marshall and Leubuscher, 1946, pp. 16–17)

This objective of 'fortifying' students through developing and using particular forms of professional education has been

a primary concern of, and reason for, all social work education. In the words of Roger Wilson, the then Head of the
Social Studies Department at Hull University:

> nobody gets such a bellyful of life fired at pointblank
> range as the social worker, and because it is only by
> education that some pattern can be injected into the res-
> ponses to the experience and so become a new integrated
> and creative experience, it is important that, of all people,
> the social worker should be well educated.

> (Wilson, 1949, p. 354)

The crucial question here is: what kind of education? As I
have argued in detail elsewhere (Jones, 1978, 1979), the history of social work education can be read as a history of a
constant struggle to implant in the neophyte professionals
a particular world-view and concomitant styles of practice
which not only do not challenge prevailing dominant social
arrangements and values but actually support and sustain
them. In this process social work educators, who could be
considered as the principal guardians of the profession, have
turned *selectively* (Heraud, 1970, 1972; Leonard, 1966)
to the social, psychological and medical sciences in order to
legitimate and give authority to their partial and often
uncritical orientation.

TRAINING OR EDUCATION?

The deeply held feeling that without a coherent, well-estab-
lished, and authoritative social philosophy social workers
would be unable to sustain the pressures of work amidst
poverty was one of the key reasons behind the COS's decision
to switch from reliance on apprenticeship modes of *training*
to formal social work *education*. According to the COS the
apprenticeship approach of providing new workers with
direct practical experience under the supervision of more
experienced charity visitors was undeniably important, but
was insufficient in its capacity to instil in new workers the
insulating principles which inspired all 'good social work'.

Thus, according to Holman, 'Training which is confined to an office is of real value and should in no case be omitted, but alone it may leave the learner rather limited by routine than raised to the fuller freedom given by an understanding of root principles' (1914, p. 83).

Helen Bosanquet maintained that apprenticeship alone was 'rather dangerous in several ways' as a method of training, because it will result in the visitor tending to 'work by dead rule instead of by living principles' (1900, p. 52). This move from training to social work education by the COS was thus not some self-evident sign of a 'natural' thirst for knowledge, but rather an essentially political process for the purposes of fortifying the conviction of social workers and imbuing them with the principles of the COS's idealist and individualistic ideology at a time when such ideas were under pressure. It was with these considerations that the COS's School of Sociology developed a model of social work education and training in 1903 which still holds to this day: namely, that students should spend half of their time in the 'academic' study of social work's underlying principles and theory, and the other half undertaking practical work under supervision.

Consequently, in terms of making 'the social worker a wholly safe and effective person to engage in the tasks which fall to his lot' (Karpf, 1931, p. vii), two principal processes can be identified: on the one hand, there is the actual organisation of the social work agency and its hierarchical management structure which attempts to regulate and control social workers' daily activities with clients; and on the other hand, there is social work education which both attempts to regulate access to the occupation through an intricate system of selection and then also tries to forge a particular perspective in those whom it deems are suitable.

Neither of these two processes of regulation has been static in the development of social work. Moreover, there has been considerable concern expressed about the nature of the relationship between social work education and the local authority social services departments. One strand of this anxiety has related to the efficacy of social work education as a means of social worker socialisation and of equipping social workers with the right sort of outlook for work in the state system.

RADICALISM AND POLITICISATION

There has been a growing body of opinion which has asserted that social work education has been in part responsible for the increasing politicisation and radicalism of social workers. In other words, rather than producing social workers who will meet the requirements of the employing agency, which in Britain is predominantly the local authority social services departments, some social work courses have been accused of producing workers who, to say the least, are 'difficult' employees. This sentiment was particularly apparent during the 1978–9 social workers' strike when in a number of the strike-bound authorities claims were made that one of the causes of social worker militancy was the influence of left-wing teachers on social work courses. Thus, in a letter to David Ennals, the Labour Minister of State then responsible, Anthony Steen, the Conservative MP for Wavertree, Liverpool, maintained that one of the reasons why 'those dedicated to the deprived have turned against them' was in part the consequence of a continued flow of 'indoctrination by militant left-wing and Marxist lecturers on social work training courses' (*Liverpool Echo*, 17 October 1978). Similarly in Birmingham, another strike area, and one where many social workers had been active in campaigning against the local authority's cuts policy in the personal social services, the council considered drawing up a blacklist of social work courses from which the authority was not prepared to employ students. The following was reported in *Social Work Today*:

> Councillor Banner Adkins, chairman of Birmingham social services committee, would give no details of the blacklist but said that information was being sought in an attempt to connect the courses with recent protests over social services policy in the city. Councillor Adkins was reported in the Birmingham *Evening Mail* as saying, 'I think the universities are very much to blame for all this. We spend about £6,000 to send a social worker for two years' training and at some universities they come under political influence. We have known that this goes on at certain universities like Warwick.'

(*Social Work Today*, 14 November 1978, p. 3)

The Gould Report of 1977 was also a powerful source of support for such claims, warning of the dangers of 'Marxist penetration in higher education', and drawing particular attention to social work and teacher-training courses. For Gould, 'subversion' in these areas was especially worrying as both social workers and teachers were key figures in the state's ideological apparatus and were supposed to be guardians of the social trust, capable of developing and encouraging the right sort of social values and attitudes among those such as clients and children who were deemed to be in need of such socialisation. However, the assertions made about this supposed contamination were undoubtedly exaggerated, and reflected a common method of scapegoating the Left for events which were unpalatable to the state and the bourgeoisie.

Nevertheless, these accusations do reflect a mounting anxiety about the growing politicisation and radicalism of social workers, and this has created many problems for both social work education and for the employing authorities. To some extent social work courses have borne the brunt of these anxieties on at least two gounds: the first being that some of the subjects taught on social work courses encourage radicalism; and the second being that social work courses have failed to siphon off those considered to be unsuitable for employment in the occupation.

Taking this second point first, there has been a growing awareness over recent years that there have been major changes in the characteristics of social workers. From at least the mid-1960s there has been a general consensus in the social work literature that those coming into social work are of a 'different stuff' from earlier generations of social workers. The differences mentioned have been varied, but they include such factors as the fact that they tend to be younger, more articulate, more critical, less passive, and so on. Thus whereas in the past many of those entering social work already had a clear and firm predisposition to the ideals of the occupation, those now entering social work cannot be assumed to be so clearly inspired by what Mays termed the 'strong tradition in the middle classes for what may be termed public service — an old imperial *noblesse oblige* approach to life' (1967), p. 204).

Consequently, social work courses, constituting one of the most important avenues into the occupation, were by the end of the 1960s confronting a more active and critical student body and facing considerable difficulties in coping. According to Rankin:

> the most vocal and dynamic of the new recruits to social work are anti-professionalism with its inbuilt paternalism and inequalities. They do not see themselves as skilled experts dispensing therapy to social misfits, but as community workers where the client is not longer the sick person but the sick society.
>
> (Rankin, 1970, p. 21)

Yet again, however, there has been a tendency among some commentators to regard the radicalisation of significant numbers of social work students as being wholly derived from 'external' socialist sources. In fact, the changing character of social work students and their tendency to be more critical and questioning of social work's purpose is much more complex than this. Indeed, a whole variety of factors have been at play in bringing about these changes, including the development of the women's movement and radical feminism, anarchism, the emergence of powerful new critiques and ideas in psychiatry (e.g. Laing's work) and deviancy theory, as well as other factors relating to the disillusionment among many young liberals and social democrats within the middle classes concerning the evident failures of the welfare state to effect any radical improvement in eradicating poverty and bring about a more egalitarian distribution of wealth and opportunity.

In other words, social work was having to cope with a general upsurge of oppositional activities and movements particularly within the liberal middle class. It was not merely a socialist-inspired opposition, as some writers have suggested, but a whole wave of alternative cultures that included rock music, squatting, anti-Vietnam protests, drugs, communes, and so on. For social work this oppositional culture had a relatively important presence among many liberal arts and social science students in universities and higher education generally. For these students the growth of the personal social services and the demand for more social workers in the mid-1960s and early 1970s offered major employment possibilities. Social work, as Pearson (1973, pp. 213ff) discovered, did not only seem to be an appropriately relevant career for individuals with social science degrees, but with its emphasis on helping and 'working with people' seemed more attractive than working in a large multinational corporation. As Cowley argued, 'these professionals do have a liberal-humanist ideology which embraces the desire to serve others, and in practice the state offers far more attractive employment to politically conscious young people than does industry or commerce, where their involvement in exploiting and manipulating workers is more direct and obvious' (1977, p. 92).

Thus social work, and education courses in particular, were now having to deal with a quite different generation of recruits, some of whom had been politicised in the wide-ranging counter-culture, some of whom had turned to the revolutionary socialist groups, and many of whom looked to social work not as a professional vocation, but rather as a job which may not be too alienating. Therefore, it was not so much that social work courses had radicalised students, but that more critical students were coming into social work. The problem for social work education has been its inability to implement an effective selection procedure which would ensure that such students did not gain access to the courses in the first place, and its failure to dispel the criticisms of the students and to socialise them into the mainstream culture of social work. Certainly, by the late 1960s, despite the fact that through the Seebohm reorganisation and the 1969 Children and Young Persons Act the government had pledged its faith in the legitimacy of social work as a discrete activity in its own right, central tenents of social work theory and practice were under considerable strain. Writing in 1972, Katherine Kendall noted that

schools of social work throughout the world are passing through a period of intense preoccupation with the purpose of social work in society . . . social work education is in trouble in its essence and on its boundaries.

(Kendall, 1972, p. 6)

With the so-called 'rediscovery of poverty' and the important writings of Townsend and Abel-Smith and others indicating that large sectors of the population are condemned to poverty, not through personal inadequacy but through the unequal and unfair structure of social and economic institutions, combined with specific attacks on the futility of casework, the optimism and confidence which typified social work in the 1950s (and which was so well caricatured by Wootton (1959) for its pomposity) were no longer present by the late 1960s. The consequence, as Carmichael noted, was that while 'core teaching on courses remained the same in substance', the '*conviction* on the part of teachers sagged in the face of the students' increasing emphasis on the importance of poverty and society'. And she continued:

To be a Freudian or neo-Freudian was increasingly to be designated as rather unsophisticated; there wasn't time to do casework anyway. The capacity to be angry was in fashion, the capacity to make a relationship less important. The theoretical input on courses was maintained but whether because of conviction or pressure of work the effect on practice became more dubious. By the 1970s it was being claimed that social work was no more than friendship and helping people to get their rights.

(Carmichael, 1976, p. 16)

Not only were social work education courses having difficulty in implementing an effective selection strategy, but they were also facing a major crisis of confidence. Thus, lacking in conviction and unable to answer many of the points raised by students, the capacity of social work courses to contribute to the regulation of social workers through professional socialisation was being increasingly questioned by local authorities. Furthermore, local authorities also began to question some of the teaching, particularly in the contributory social science disciplines, which was provided on the courses. One subject which has caused both local authorities and the social work leadership concern was sociology. Sociology, since the beginnings of formal social work education, has been regarded as an essential theoretical discipline for intending social workers. However, for social work, the kind of sociology which has been regarded as important has been that which supports and justifies its particular approach to the problems of the working-class poor (Leonard, 1966, pp. 22—3). Thus, in an analysis of examination papers given to social work students, Heraud discovered that virtually all the sociology questions were on family-related issues, such as child-rearing and socialisation, and the relationships between the nuclear and extended family types. It appears, he wrote, 'that sociology, to those who set the papers, is mainly concerned with questions about the family and that this is the main reason for having sociology in the course' (1967, p. 14). He also added that there was a 'lack of concern with the whole field of social control' and that the 'overall perspective was eclectic and functionalist' (1967, pp. 15, 16).

However, by the late 1960s there had been important radical shifts within whole segments of sociology, with the result that on some social work courses students were now receiving a much more critical education. Of particular concern to many professional social work tutors was the impact on students of the new radical deviance material:

Current theories in the sociology of deviance pose the greatest threat of all to social work students, with their clear message that society creates deviants for its own ends and that social workers are part of the system of social control, are used to create and amplify deviance rather than improve the lot of the deviant. The ideas of writers like Matza, Becker, Cicourel are intellectually fascinating and persuasive but quite ominous for the social workers.

(Munday, 1972, p. 4)

And, according to Wilson, who lectured sociology to social work students, this type of teaching was dangerous in that it led to students feeling confused and despondent about their professional vocation; 'Such an accusation cannot be dismissed lightly. The dangers of undermining the professional commitments of novices in the field parallel those of putting a viper in the cradle of an infant'. (1974, p. 9). That such critical teaching can take place on social work courses at all is in part indicative of a certain lack of control by the social work leadership and the employing state authorities over course content and structure. By being located in the higher education structure — a choice of venue made by social work for professional enhancement (Younghusband, 1947, pp. 172—3) — social work courses are to some extent bound by the traditions of liberal education and academic freedom. This tradition has consequently made it difficult for social work courses to control closely the inputs made by those teachers of contributory disciplines such as sociology, psychology and social policy who, in the main, are not professional social workers, and who may not share the professional staff's objectives for the course.

But the difficulty for social work in preventing contamination does not lie solely in its lack of control over the non-professional academic content of courses — although CCETSW is currently attempting to establish this (Wright, 1977) — but rather in the more fundamental challenge of a wide range of critical social science theories and insights which make greater sense of the domain of social work and the problems social workers have to deal with. Thus the influence of some aspects of the new deviancy perspectives, critical social policy and psychology, feminist writings on the family, etc., derives from this capacity to make more sense of the world than does traditional social work knowledge. Although attempts to control 'non-professional' teachers on social work courses may yield some benefits to social work in muting certain challenging insights, it hardly promises any long-term impact, for ideas and theories which shed understanding on complex social and personal problems are not possible to censure in this manner. The problem confronting social work from these so-called demoralising perspectives is considerable, and possibly impossible for it to contend with. After all, its idealist and individualistic foundations leave it with little room to manoeuvre.

CONCLUSION

Over the past decade or so professional social work courses of the CQSW type have come increasingly under fire. Criticisms have been varied, and although the main challenge has come from local authorities there have also been queries raised from within social work education itself. Martin Davies, Professor of Social Work at the University of East Anglia, has, for example, been at the forefront in criticising professional social work courses for being too lax in their assessment procedures (see Cypher, 1979; Brandon and Davies, 1979). He has also expressed concern about the role of academic inputs such as sociology for their tendency to produce 'critical, questioning, and even sceptical graduates' (Davies, 1981, p. 19). Indeed, Davies has articulated many of the doubts which have been expressed by the local authorities: namely, that CQSW courses have tended to produce difficult employees who are apparently well versed in their criticisms of state social work but have little to offer in terms of practice. The solution proposed by Davies includes a radical reassessment of the professional course content and above all a greater willingness of university departments to work with the employing authorities in the design of courses. It is certainly clear from his writings that Davies is deeply worried that local authorities may well turn away from the universities unless radical changes are made. And there are certainly grounds for such a position. In a letter to *Social Work Today* Mary Hope, the training officer for Hillingdon Social Services, remarked that

Regarding the appropriateness of the training job, it is almost universally acknowledged that the CQSW prepares students for a task that it is not possible to do within the current local authority social services organisation. There is also the problem that many courses omit basic knowledge and skills required by social workers.

(*Social Work Today*, 25 January 1977, p. 26)

While note should be taken of the various details of the criticisms that have been levelled at professional social work courses, it is also important that the major theme which underpins much of the challenge should be recognised. Broadly stated this refers to the growing disillusionment of local authorities in particular about the efficacy of social work education in achieving its traditional objectives. These include the tasks of professional socialisation; strengthening the resolve of social workers so that they can handle the pressures of working among the poor without being 'contaminated' and subverted; and generally acting as one of the most important gateways to the occupation and therefore ensuring only those deemed suitable for work are admitted. In the last decade in particular, it has become increasingly evident that many local authorities are not entirely hopeful that despite recent changes CQSW type courses can achieve these objectives alone, and as a consequence they have begun to introduce new forms of work processes and styles of education in order to exert greater control over social workers, and it is to these developments that this book now turns.

7

Difficult Employees

INTRODUCTION

Many local authority departments have found it increasingly difficult to make social workers conform to their policies and priorities, and in particular they complain about a general lack of loyalty to the agency by many of their employees. What is at issue here is possibly one of the most pervasive and difficult contradictions which makes social work such a fraught activity for the state. For what has occurred over the past thirty-five years of social work's growth and expansion, with increasing rapidity especially since reorganisation in the early 1970s, has been a widening gulf between the professional objectives and concerns of social work and the state's requirements for the personal social services. In other words, the relationship between social work and the state has itself become increasingly strained.

There have been profound changes taking place in the character of state social work. In particular, the local authority social services departments which are the main locations of social work practice have been gradually reshaped. Thus instead of being preoccupied with the treatment and rehabilitation of clients, the focus of their work is now much more on containing a wide range of problems and of acting as a servicing agency for the welfare apparatus as a whole. According to Bill Jordan, 'social workers will be needed more, not less, by government policies, but their role will increasingly be required to be that of rationing scarce resources and exercising social control' (1981, p. 9). These changes have meant that many social workers now have to spend most of their time trying to juggle with the impossible demands of a large caseload. The reality for most social workers is that their day-to-day work involves them in rushing from one emergency to another: a threatened disconnection here, an eviction there, down to the police station, and on top of all this they have to manage the badgering over the telephone from other official bodies demanding action of one sort or another with respect to particular individuals. In other words, the actual texture of contemporary social work practice in most local authorities is rapidly moving away from the professional ideals of the activity, or at least away from those ideals which are discussed in much of the social work literature.

This restructuring has brought about important changes within the structure and organisation of the state's personal social services and, in particular, demands new skills and capacities from its workers. Thus, for example, local authority social services departments expect social workers to have considerable skills in being able to liaise effectively between a whole galaxy of state and official bodies; they require workers who have a good grasp of the massive legislation which sets out the duties and obligations of the departments; and above all, given that the social services are now operationalised within large and complex bureaucracies, they demand social workers who can work in such settings, obey the instructions of managers, and of course fill in the myriad of forms and dossiers which are the lifeblood of such institutions.

The restructuring of the personal social services has had a profound effect on social workers themselves. The bureaucratisation of social services departments following the 1970 Local Authority Social Services Act has placed many extra constraints on social workers and greatly reduced the extent of their autonomy and control. Thus as Leonard has commented:

The kinds of organisations in which social workers are employed are getting bigger, especially local authority departments. As organisations increase in size, they require a central administrative structure which ensures that the activities of the members of the organisation are all directed towards the official objectives. The bureaucratic structure of a social work organisation aims at securing predictable behaviour from social workers in conformity to policy.

(Leonard 1968, p. 303)

For vast numbers of social workers, the reorganisation of the local authority departments has been experienced in the manner described by Leonard. Rather than marking a new dawn for social work, as many commentators thought (Donnison, 1968, p. 3; Kahn, 1970, p. 59), the Seebohm reorganisation has led to many social workers experiencing a marked diminution in their independence and a far greater pressure to meet the requirements of the department. As Oppenheimer noted:

Under these conditions such persons are no longer able to work at their own pace, determine the use of their talents or products, or in fact much of anything about the work place, whose owners and controllers are often far removed from them both physically and in terms of social standing.

(Oppenheimer, 1975, p. 35)

And, according to Goldberg, one of the major dilemmas now facing social workers employed by local authority social services departments 'is the almost inevitable conflict between professional independence and autonomy at field level and the hierarchical structure of bureaucracies with its long chains of command' (1974, p. 268).

Throughout many areas of social work there have been complaints from social workers who have been dismayed by their increasing inability to effect any meaningful influence over local authority policy, more so in recent years when many councils have implemented cuts in the service/provision aspects of the personal social services. These cuts make many of the tasks of social workers very much more difficult. Thus many of the clashes between social workers and their employing authorities evident during the social workers' strike have stemmed from growing professional discontent among many social workers. Many feel angry and confused about the ways in which they are burdened with mundane servicing work and at the same time are expected to manage the many crises occuring in their caseloads.

As cuts in social welfare provision, compounded by the recession, make survival more problematic for clients, so social workers have ever fewer resources to draw upon. In this context the possibility of providing a casework service for clients becomes increasingly remote: 'They are aware that lack of time makes it impossible to do the job in the way in which they have been trained and which they believe to be most effective' (Haines, 1967, p. 18); or 'those of us who fought for years to establish, maintain, and enhance sound casework practice see a marked deterioration in the service the clients receive and are appalled by what can be peddled out in the name of casework nowadays' (Pearson, 1975a, p. 42, citing Baker, *Social Work Today*, vol. 5(6), 1974). Consequently, one of the major sites of conflict within the contemporary personal social services has arisen not so much from a clearly radical perspective and politics but, for many social workers, from the way in which the relationship between social work and the state has developed. Thus the result of reorganisation in the early 1970s has been, according to one practising social worker, that if one 'tries to work on social work principles and values, this is in many ways not because of the social services departments but in spite of the department' (Parton, 1975, p. 1).

These tensions have rippled throughout social work. The word 'crisis' crops up again and again in the professional literature. The major DHSS-funded survey on social work directed by Parsloe *et al.* (1978), for example, uncovered profound professional discontent centred on the manner in which local authority personal social services were developing. Even social work tutors were querying the purposes of their courses. Stevenson, for example, cited social work teachers who now considered that 'the local authority is a most inhospitable setting for social work' and that 'negativism is the only possible attitude' for students who would be going back to 'being trodden on from a great height' (Stevenson, 1976, pp. 3, 14, 16).

Many of these complaints and anxieties arise out of the manner in which the personal social services have been restructured, and reflect a deep struggle going on within the local authorities about who is to determine the activities of social workers. Stated very starkly, the local authorities have been demanding that they are the chief arbiters and determinants of social work policy; they are the agencies charged with implementing the service, and, as their employees, social workers should be loyal to their policies and directives. The social work profession, on the other hand, while not dismissing the right of the employing authorities to be the main determinants of social workers' practice, has argued that social workers should not be regarded simply as employees. Rather, they should be viewed as professional people, who as such have an allegiance to a set of professional ideals relating to the nature of social work as well as an obligation to their employing agency. This point was made clear in a *Community Care* editorial, in which it was argued that local authorities should not expect slavish loyalty from professionally trained social workers: 'Indeed, it is part of the professional social worker's task to be in tension with the institutions of society, including those which are employing him and her. From the resulting dialectic there arises possibilities for change' (*Community Care*, 29 March 1979). Similarly, as public expenditure cuts have eaten into the capacities of social workers, so BASW has also reasserted the right of social workers to act 'professionally' and it has promised backing to those members who come into conflict with their employers as a result. According to the then General Secretary Chris Andrews, it is an

> essential part of a social worker's job to draw attention to the needs of their clients and to point to the effects of social policies upon them. The social worker is in a unique position to identify needs and to assess the impact of policies and services. It is professional negligence not to do so.

(*Social Work Today*, 4 September 1979, p. 23)

Unfortunately, BASW lacks the power to protect this dimension of professional integrity, and the struggle between the local authorities and social work over the degree of worker autonomy continues, with the local authorities gaining the upper hand. Some indication of this process can be found in the second annual report of the Central Council for Education and Training in Social Work, in which the Council discussed the attitude of employers to the different parts of the professional course:

> Emphasis on practical training in social work courses naturally comes from employers who expect social workers to be able to carry out a wide range of duties. For this they need to have acquired a great deal of local knowledge, to understand the rules and regulations of the organisations for which they work, and to be efficient in carrying out practical tasks. *From this point of view there may be a tendency to undervalue the academic disciplines that the students are being taught or even to suspect that the education they receive makes them difficult employees more concerned to change the 'system' than to get on with the job. Clearly, social work education must balance these pressures.*
>
> (February 1975, pp. 38—9, emphasis added)

This passage does give some evidence of the demands being made by local authorities. For, as CCETSW noted, local authority employers are looking for social workers who will be good employees, capable of undertaking the many practical skills which are now demanded of the personal social services, and who are loyal to their employing authority. These requirements were also revealed in an earlier survey undertaken by the Council for Training in Social Work — one of the forerunners of CCETSW — when they inquired of Chief Officers what qualities they looked for and welcomed in newly qualified social workers: 'those they rated most highly were concern, reliability, ability to use community resources and ability for good relations with colleagues in the department' (CTSW, 1971, p. 21). Most of these qualities relate to good labour discipline. Apart from the quality of 'concern' there was no mention of those qualities which are related to the professional ideals of social work, which stress, say, an ability to forge purposeful therapeutic relationships with clients. In the changing local authority context it would appear that employers do not welcome those social workers who are overly inspired by the professional ideals of the occupation. Indeed, it is becoming increasingly clear that some of the most difficult employees for the local authority are those social workers who insist upon being regarded and treated as autonomous professionals, with certain rights to dictate the pace and nature of their work and the freedom to criticise their employers if need be.

These issues and debates have been reflected within social work education in the development of Certificate in Social Service (CSS) courses since 1975. These courses do not supplant the CQSW courses but run alongside them, and it appears that there are increasing numbers of local authorities which prefer this form of training. The CSS is a form of in-service training. Employees are released from their jobs for one or two days a week to attend their local college. Unlike the CQSW, the CSS is a locally devised system of training in which the local authority has a major role in determining the course content. For employers, the CSS has many advantages over the CQSW and meets their demands for a more technocratic and pragmatic training. As Liddiard and Paynter argued in a paper to a seminar of Directors, the CSS has great advantages over the CQSW in that it concentrates on training people 'to do the job asked of them' (1978, p. 16). Apart from being a form of training which does not encourage the students to regard themselves as 'virtuoso' professionals, and as well as enabling the local authority to have a far greater say over course content and design, the CSS also has the great advantage of being cheaper than seconding students on to CQSW courses. An aspect of this cheapness is that, in being locally based and designed, the CSS does not have the same 'marketability' as the CQSW. Thus whereas the CQSW enables social workers to have a considerable degree of mobility the same cannot be said of the CSS, for a CSS course fashioned to meet the needs of one local authority may not be suitable or sufficiently relevant to another. Thus, although it is too early to determine accurately, it seems that the CSS will reduce social worker mobility — a factor, of course, not unrelated to the power of managerial control.

The reasons why professionalism among social workers should be such a problem for a restructured personal social services are due to the strains it occasions for the local authority bureaucracy and the ease with which this state agency can fulfil its duties, especially in the context of cuts in public expenditure and its departure from the traditional rehabilitative and caring objectives of professional social work. In this changing situation social services departments do not welcome a labour force comprising of 'virtuoso' professionals who claim the right to some autonomy and self-direction on the grounds that they 'know' what clients require and should be left to deliver the service. Employers certainly do not want to be confronted by their own employees criticising them on professional grounds, which has become a familiar feature in many departments. Thus many social workers have expressed increasing disquiet about the manner in which they feel that they are being deprofessionalised within local authorities. Among the issues raised are feelings of powerlessness within the large bureaucracies where policy decisions are handed down to basic grade field-workers without any consultation (Parsloe *et al.*, 1978, p. 430). Moreover, increasing numbers of social workers are realising that many of the policy decisions that are being passed down to them have more to do with bureaucratic efficiency and perspectives than with the needs and problems of providing an appropriate service to clients. As Leonard has observed:

> Although the reorganisation of the services has enabled professional social workers to take up senior organisational positions, the resulting structure presents a number of potential problems in the path of professional development. In many of the new structures authority is once again based on organisational position rather than specialised professional knowledge and basic conflicts continue to emerge between bureaucratic and professional cultures.

> (Leonard, 1973, p. 107)

THE DAWN HOUSE INCIDENT

A clear example of the nature of these conflicts and the manner in which local authorities are attempting to exert greater control over social workers arose in Birmingham, where a large number of social workers had been campaigning against the council's decision to close a number of children's homes as part of the expenditure cuts. The Birmingham Children's Defence Campaign (BCDC), which co-ordinated the social workers' opposition, asserted that its criticism of the council's decision rested largely on its 'professional' judgement that such economies were damaging to the children concerned and were preventing the provision of a necessary service.

In this dispute the relationship between the employing authority and its social workers became most strained over the use of Dawn House, a hostel for the mentally handicapped. A large number of social workers wanted the hostel to be converted into an assessment/rehabilitation unit for the mentally disordered, but this was rejected by Birmingham's social services committee. This decision provoked a public demonstration which included a number of social workers, and this involvement by social workers in a demonstration against their employers in turn outraged the council, who immediately appointed an inquiry team to investigate the actions of the protesting social workers.

The conclusions of this inquiry team, which comprised a barrister (Francis Allen) and the former director of Leeds Social Services (Bill Freeman), are highly significant in demonstrating the manner in which local authorities are increasingly regarding their social workers. Its principal conclusion was a condemnation of the social workers' actions in publicly demonstrating against their employer. According to the team's report, a social worker is first and foremost an officer of the local government, and as such their first duty was to show 'undivided allegiance' to the authority. The report added:

The duty to give undivided allegiance must plainly mean: (a) in his work and in his use of council facilities and

property to obey all lawful instructions and loyally to
implement all lawful decisions of his employers; (b) never
to allow his work to be affected by private interest or
improper motives; (c) never to give cause for even suspicion
of bribery or corruption.

(cited in *Social Work Today*, 27 February, 1979)

The report continued that social workers have a right to
express opposition to employers, but that this must be done
through the appropriate managerial structures. On no account
was it permissible for social workers to oppose policies
publicly.

The Dawn House incident is by no means unique. As more
and more cuts have been made in social service budgets,
increasing numbers of social workers have come into conflict
with their employing authorities. For many of these social
workers it has been a question of protesting about what they
see as policies which are detrimental to their clients and
which are opposed to the objectives of social work. One of
the responses from the local authorities has been that adopted
in Birmingham, namely insisting that social workers are above
all local authority employees, and that as such they should
be unquestioningly loyal to the council's policies, and bound
accordingly by their contracts of employment.

But councils are not finding it at all easy to control social
workers in this manner. For example, Councillor Banner
Adkins, the chairman of Birmingham social services committee, admitted that 'his most difficult task since becoming
chairman over two years ago had been to impress upon all
members of staff that they are first of all local government
officers who are engaged under a code of behaviour' (*Social
Work Today*, 27 February 1979, p. 11). Many local authorities now make a great point of stressing the nature of social
workers' conditions of service and are following the recommendations of the Birmingham inquiry which suggested that
'staff should be periodically reminded of their allegiance'
(*Social Work Today*, 23 January 1979, p. 4). It is now
possible to read in the professional journals of incidents in
which social workers have either been dismissed or disciplined

not because they acted unprofessionally but because they failed to show undivided allegiance to their employers. In Bradford, for example, an area officer was reprimanded because he allowed a local residents' group to publish their own community newspaper which was critical of council policy from a community advice centre under his control. It was stated that

> Social workers in Bradford were not prepared to talk publicly about the case last week for fear of reprisals. One who has asked to remain anonymous told *SWT*: 'This case has very severe implications for all area officers in Bradford. It is designed to stop council staff getting involved in activities that are remotely critical of council policy.'

> (*Social Work Today*, 20 March 1979, p. 3)

FORMS, DOSSIERS AND THE PROLETARIANISATION OF SOCIAL WORK

The changes in the labour process which are currently under way within local authority social services departments are not being implemented through new legislation or through dramatic and immediate changes of policy. Rather, it is a gradual process of change which appears to be slowly ensuring greater employer control over the majority of social services workers. (Clearly there will be some who benefit from some of these changes, particularly those in managerial and supervisory roles.) In the main the major thrust of these changes appears to be in the direction of reducing further the already limited professional autonomy of social workers by introducing measures which will ensure more effective worker conformity to the policies of the employing agency. Such a process is by no means peculiar to social work, and writers such as Braverman (1974) have identified similar processes at work across the labour market, particularly in areas of skilled labour. The name given to these developments is that of 'proletarianisation'. For many social workers proletarianisation' has become an increasing feature of their experience of work within a local authority social services department and especially as a consequence of increasing bureaucratic controls over their work.

Social workers experience this changing character of the personal social services not only through the type of work they are expected to do with clients but also in the manner in which they are expected to work within their agencies. An important part of that experience concerns the increasing amount of paperwork they are expected to deal with; paperwork both in the nature of case records and in the number of official forms and reports they are supposed to complete. That social workers spend up to a third of their working week in their offices undertaking bureaucratic paperwork provides a very clear indication of the significance of this aspect of contemporary state social work. Yet there has been little critical attention paid to this aspect of social work, which is surprising, for the increase in forms and dossiers of all kinds has in part stemmed from, and reflects, the changing character of state social work which has necessitated ever closer supervision and control over individual social workers.

All those with experience of local authority social services departments will know of the importance which is attached to the filling in of forms of all kinds and to maintaining records. In Gateshead social services department, which is by no means untypical, social workers have, until recently, had ninety-six different forms and documents to cope with which cover the various aspects of the department's work. Many social workers regard such tasks as irksome and irritating because of the time it consumes and the way in which it reduces the time they can spend with clients. But for the department these completed forms and records are its very lifeblood; they constitute one of its most crucial sources of information on what is being done by its social workers. Indeed, it often seems that social services managements are more concerned about receiving the appropriately completed form on time than with virtually any other activity, and that most departments look to their completed forms and dossiers as the end-product. Moreover, the efficiency and effectiveness of social workers and their teams are judged almost entirely on the degree to which they keep their records and forms up to date.

But the growth in the number of forms and the importance which is attached to them is not simply a reflection of the manner in which the personal social services have expanded, nor are they some inevitable byproduct of bureaucratisation, though both these factors have contributed to the process. Rather, their expansion also reflects the long-standing concern to regulate the activities of social workers in their direct contact with clients. As noted earlier, the character of social work demands that a deeply personal and individualised relationship between the social worker and the client should be forged if there is to be any possibility for treatment. This has entailed a method of work in which it appears that social workers are left largely on their own with clients. This interface of social worker and client has been one of the main sites of professional autonomy, and the space and freedom which it allows for the social worker to create a relationship with a client has been one of the main attractions of social work for many people, whether they be diehard caseworkers or radicals and socialists.

However, from the time of the COS, there have always been some restrictions on this degree of freedom open to social workers. One of the main purposes of social worker supervision has traditionally been to keep a check on the activities of social workers with their clients, and to ensure that the appropriate relationships and interventions are implemented. However, there are certain restrictions on supervision, such as its retrospective character and its reliance on the social worker to report accurately, which make it a relatively permissive form of control. One cannot help feel that as doubts have grown, particularly recently, about the 'trustworthiness' of social workers and their general capacity to act loyally in the interests of the local authority, so social services managements have sought to introduce new methods for controlling the interventions of social workers.

Certainly, the growth in the number of forms in social services departments has had a considerable influence in directing such intervention and has been a major factor in the routinisation of social work and the curtailment of professional autonomy. More often than not in contemporary social services departments many of the contacts between social workers and their clients are now to some extent determined by an official form. Thus social workers are rarely free agents who can determine for themselves the nature and parameters of the social worker/client relationship. In a northern county's social services department, for example, a social worker setting out to visit a new referral is armed with 'Initial Investigation Form SS 26'. This form, to be completed by the social worker, sets out the issues to be covered with the client. Apart from the purely factual information, the sections to be completed include 'family efficiency (home conditions, economic practices, quality of relationships, emotional atmosphere)'; financial circumstances, followed by a family history including 'individual behaviour and adjustment (i.e. describe the individual family members, give a brief sketch of appearance, personality and behaviour, drawing on school reports, psychological summaries, police and probation records, etc., as well as your own observations of capacities and limitations. Response of clients to social worker)'. Thus the demands of the form can have a significant bearing on the nature of the actual contact between the social worker and the client, and if followed, can control at least part of the social worker's actions.

In recent years there have been further changes in the nature of the forms and record-keeping which have taken this process of control further. A most important factor in this process has been the introduction of the computerisation of forms and records. That this has led to further restrictions on social worker autonomy arises from the manner in which computerised record-keeping prefers information which is expressed very simply, either by a tick or cross against some category, rather than a long interpretative passage from the social worker who tries to capture the complexity of the issues involved. Many of the forms now used contain lists of characteristics and circumstances which the social worker is expected to tick off where appropriate and which leave little or no space for qualifying statements. The following example

is taken from the form used by Durham social services
department with regard to housing referrals:

FAMILY FUNCTIONING

Finance

HUSBAND

Poor health	
Workshy	
Poor provider	
Inadequate	
Leaves management to wife	

WIFE

Poor health	
Poor manager	
Priority personal pleasure	
Generally inadequate	
Does her best	

Care of children

HUSBAND

Interested	
Involved	
Punitive	
Supportive	
Inconsistent	

WIFE

Interested	
Involved	
Overprotective	
Punitive	
Supportive	
Overwhelmed	
Inconsistent	

HUSBAND AND WIFE

United front	

As the example illuminates, there is no room for manoeuvre
available to the social worker, who is compelled to tick the
appropriate box, and no more. In this instance the client
stands to receive a most damning assessment given that all the
categories except about four are negative and moralistic.
Furthermore, this kind of form also illustrates the manner
in which local authority practices are fast eroding one of the
most potentially progressive features of social work, namely
its holistic approach to clients, whereby the social worker

attempts to consider all the issues which affect a client's position and problems. This kind of form (with its stark list of categories) does not allow a social worker to develop such a meaningful perspective on clients, and is certainly no aid to those clients and social workers who attempt to put forward the best possible argument in order to ensure that the client receives some of the discretionary resources available.

COMPUTERISATION

Many social services departments are now considering installing a fully computerised system. The system which seems most likely to be introduced is that developed by ICL and tested in Gateshead. The installation of a fully integrated computer system has many advantages for a local authority social services department intent upon securing a disciplined work-force. It is noteworthy that, despite the extent of the cuts in many departments' budgets, plans are advanced in many areas for the introduction of a computer system which will cost in the region of £250,000 to install.

In the unpublished ICL report on the Gateshead system it was made clear that computerisation can bring many advantages to the local authority. It was stressed, for example, that it leads to much improved labour management. In Gateshead computerisation reduced the time field social workers spent on administrative tasks from 25 per cent of their working week to between 12 and 15 per cent. It also reduced the number of official forms and documents used from ninety-six to thirteen. Reductions on this scale can obviously permit social services departments to reduce the number of their servicing and clerical staff. And if the experience of other industries is noted, the amount of time saved through computerisation will be used by managements to justify increased caseloads, the freezing of vacant posts and even redundancies, on the grounds that social workers have more time available. Thus, although many social workers might initially welcome a development which seemingly reduced the time they had to spend in the office on record and form-filling, the introduction of computers could well be against their interests because the time saved will not be *their* time to reallocate as they please.

This point is reinforced by the ICL report's constant reiteration that one of the great advantages of the system is that it enables managers to have more control over what social workers are doing and allows them greater scope for assessing what is happening in the authority. As the report noted, by a flick of a switch a social work manager can now gain a complete breakdown of an individual social worker's caseload, highlighting, for example, review dates and resources allocated. Whereas in the past this sort of detailed information was difficult for managers to retrieve from a mass of case files and papers, the computer system allows for instant and complete information. As ICL observed, this access is 'of great benefit to both senior and principal social workers in their respective supervisory roles'.

Thus, sitting at a terminal, social work managers will now be able to identify immediately the total caseloads of their social workers, and in particular identify those social workers who appear to distribute more than is expected in the way of material resources. In a cost-conscious social services department one wonders what will happen to those social workers who are seen as big spenders. If the experience of labour processes in the social security system is any guide (Hill, 1969), the knowledge that the department is closely supervising relief-giving activities may well have a salutary effect on social workers, especially with the possibility that promotion could in part become dependent on the worker's careful use of material resources.

Computerisation also permits other labour-disciplining processes to be introduced more effectively. According to the report, 'the system brings about a *much needed discipline* to case recording; no longer can case details or requests for service be scribbled onto any piece of paper' (emphasis added). Here again can be glimpsed the problems local authorities have confronted in their attempt to inculcate certain basic labour routines among their social workers. But if computerisation is to work, it demands the total co-operation of the social workers to feed in the appropriate information in the prescribed manner. This is clearly one

of its weaknesses, for although it is trying to make management more efficient and is exposing social workers to ever
tighter supervision, it still depends upon social workers
co-operating in the process. The ICL report recognised that
contradiction and was forced to resort to moral exhortation
as the means of ensuring compliance by arguing that the only
people who would suffer from any social worker resistance
would be the clients themselves:

> As with any computer system certain set procedures have
> to be adhered to and staff soon accept that if their client
> is to receive a specific resource/service the appropriate
> document must be completed and submitted to the system
> in the prescribed manner.

This is the first time in the report that any mention is made
of how clients may benefit by the introduction of computers.
Indeed, it is more likely that the consequences for clients will
be ambiguous. Those clients who have 'done well' in terms of
securing material help from their social workers — cash aid
under the 1963 Act, aids and adaptations, and so on — will
now be easily identifiable under the ICL system. For through

> the use of a real time conversational system, field work
> staff have almost instant access to up to date comprehen-
> sive information relating to a client. Giving them a concise
> pen picture of which departmental resources/services, etc.,
> the client is currently in receipt of, which resources they
> require and which resources they have had in the past.

Thus whereas in the past a social worker could exploit the
mass of paperwork which accumulated on clients in order to
gain as many resources as possible from their own and other
council departments, the advent of computerisation blocks off
this possible line of 'banditry' (Pearson, 1975). Thus some
clients could find it more difficult to secure material help.
However, for most clients the dangers of computerisation will
be in the threat it poses for their privacy. The computer
system devised by ICL is capable of storing immense quanti-
ties of information on clients. The code list on 'present and

presenting problems' contains twenty different classifications; list 52 ('Referral Agent') contains thirty-seven different possibilities; for children in care there are seventy admission reasons; and so on. Within the ICL report, the protection of information stored on clients is not discussed, and instead it would seem to ICL that there is much to be said for the information being available throughout the local authority. Thus they talk of the system as enabling family/household links to be built up by cross-referencing, both within the district/area and throughout the particular authority, 'and providing a base of data about "people" within an authority'. Given the poor record of social services departments in maintaining a strict regard for client confidentiality (Brandon, 1975) and the fact that social workers lack any ultimate legal sanction for protecting the privacy of the client, there is good reason to be anxious about the effects of computerisation.

Before leaving computerisation, it is worth again stressing that despite the problems that this development could pose for many social workers and clients, there are also potential difficulties facing those local authorities which install and use such new technology. For example, it is by no means certain that the new system will gain the total co-operation of all those workers who are supposed to work the system. This could pose many problems for a system that requires a high degree of worker co-operation in order to work efficiently. Social workers could also through collective action demand such conditions of client privacy and confidentiality — which are after all appropriate and legitimate 'professional' demands — so as to prevent a local authority from investing in computerisation or greatly inhibiting its value and use. Furthermore, social workers could also press the local authority to ensure that the computer (if installed) is used to collect and collate information which might well be embarrassing to the local authority: for example, the unmet demand for home helps, meals on wheels, nursery places, services and resources for the handicapped and the ill, evictions, fuel disconnections, etc. In other words, the computerisation of social services departments could provide new possibilities as well as new problems for progressive social workers and clients.

THE STRUGGLE CONTINUES

The purpose of this chapter has been to demonstrate that one of the key factors determining the nature of personal social services organisation and practice has been the issue of controlling and regulating social workers. As noted, this problem has changed over the years. Some themes have remained, such as the perennial problem of how to prevent social workers 'going native', or taking the client's side, but other features have changed. For example, it is virtually impossible to find in any of the professional literature produced before the early 1960s any mention of problems with students whether it related to their commitment to social work or to their politics. Yet the last decade has seen a rumbling anxiety throughout many local authorities and on many social work courses about social workers who come out of training 'armed with little red books on the thoughts of Chairman Mao' (Coventry councillor, cited in *Social Work Today*, 27 February 1979, p. ii).

Throughout the whole of the COS period, and right up until the late 1960s, a great deal of sacrifice was required of social workers in that wages were either extremely poor or non-existent, and grants for courses were very few and small, which meant that most students had to be self-financing. But, over the past decade there has been a dramatic change and the job no longer requires such financial sacrifice. It would seem that social work has been slow to respond to these changes and to realise the extent to which they relied on this extensive self-selection of social workers. With improved career and wage structures and with better funding for courses it is no longer the case that only those who are already committed to the ideals and values of social work are going to be attracted to the occupation. Thus social work has had to adapt to a new set of problems arising out of these material changes, which has exposed deficiencies in its selection procedures and in the failure of its theoretical and ideological perspectives to win over more circumspect recruits.

Changes in the state's organisation of the personal social services has also created a new set of problems. As the local authority social services departments have moved increasingly towards operating mainly as a servicing/dustbin agency of the state, containing and masking a whole galaxy of problems as cheaply as possible, so the departments have had to try and move their social workers with them. In particular, this has involved a process of deprofessionalisation among social services staff and a general restructuring of labour. In this changed and changing context, local authorities do not welcome social workers who believe themselves to be virtuoso professionals who feel that they should have the right exclusively to control their work. On many issues a powerful professional social work culture rests uneasily within local government bureaucracies.

Thus many of the latest developments within the local authority social services, ranging from the increasing use of forms and computerisation, to the attempts to make social workers realise that they are first and foremost local government employees with a contractual obligation to maintain undivided loyalty to the employing agency, must be considered as one part of a struggle to control social workers. This struggle has heralded changes in social work education, with the emergence of new forms of training (the Certificate of Social Service); it has stimulated the development of systems theory as a major theoretical orientation within social work knowledge; it has given rise to a considerable restructuring of the labour force within social services departments; and these departments have also been compelled to consider more carefully caseload management and labour relations in general. Similarly, many of these changes have met with new forms of worker response and resistance. Growing numbers of social workers have looked to the trade-union movement rather than their own professional organisations (e.g. BASW) as a means of resisting some of the local authorities' policies. More social workers have actively participated in the work of pressure groups such as the Child Poverty Action Group, or formed their own groups as a means of fighting for better services for clients. In other words, the history of contemporary social work is characterised by this dialectical movement: changes in one area bringing about changes in another. It is a struggle which has brought gains and losses to both sides, and in the final chapter an assessment of the current situation is offered in order to determine what new possibilities are emerging from this process of restructuring that can assist in the fight for better social services in the short term, and for socialism in the long term.

8

Possibilities and Problems

TRADE UNIONISM

New possibilities and problems are emerging from the restructuring of the personal social services and the current
recession. For many, one of the most promising developments
over the last decade has been the expansion of trade unionism
among social workers. However, the joining of a trade union
by increasing numbers of social workers must be considered
carefully. It certainly should not be taken simply as reflecting
a move towards a more radical politics by all those who have
joined either NALGO or NUPE.

The growth of trade-union membership among social
workers over the past decade is a reflection of the changing
nature of the state's personal social services. The reduction
in professional autonomy and the increasing tendency for
local authorities to regard their social workers primarily
as employees have not been conducive to the promotion of
a professional consciousness. Indeed, the recent experience
of working within local authorities has compelled many
social workers to view themselves more as waged labour than
professionals, and it is this development which has been a
crucial influence in the growth of trade unionism. Furthermore, many of the problems confronting social workers in
the restructured social services have been those which are
appropriate to a trade union rather than a professional body
such as BASW. Thus social workers have looked increasingly
towards the trade-union movement as being the most appropriate organisation to represent them in their negotiations

with management over day-to-day issues of work organisation as well as salaries and general conditions of service.

While it is difficult to gauge accurately the numbers involved, it could be argued that a large number of social workers have joined NALGO or NUPE not in a spirit of solidarity with the working class, or from a standpoint which sees many new possibilities emerging from being a part of organised labour, but rather because the trade unions offer the best means for securing better wages and improved working conditions. One senses that some social workers wish they could avoid such union membership. For these social workers there is a sense of considerable disappointment in the performance of the professional association, BASW. Although it has a monopolistic position, being the only professional body for field social workers with some influence — for example, it has representatives on CCETSW and is asked for its opinions by government when drawing up legislation — BASW has been unable to capture a large and enthusiastic membership. Throughout the 1970s, it has stumbled from one financial crisis to another as its membership has either declined or remained static. For many social workers, BASW is regarded as weak and too remote and out of touch with developments in the work-place. And by having no strong presence in the local authorities it has been unable to fight effectively for social workers' interests.

Thus for a substantial number of social workers, membership of a trade union has been a consequence of the weakness and ineffectiveness of their professional body. There have been attempts to revamp the organisation and in the mid- to late 1970s BASW itself actively promoted the formation of the British Union of Social Workers (BUSW). BUSW is very much the attempt of BASW to become more relevant to the needs of social workers who are now faced with a more hostile local authority environment. By being restricted only to social workers rather than other state employees, it is argued that BUSW would be able to represent social workers' interests more effectively than NALGO or NUPE, and would be able to maintain a professional rather than a labourist dimension in its negotiations with management.

Thus for those social workers who are uneasy about being

a member of a TUC-affiliated union and who are attracted to such initiatives as BUSW, unionisation is more of a response to the way they feel the departments are attempting to deprofessionalise their role. In many ways it is a rearguard action which is attempting to reverse certain deskilling processes within social services bureaucracies. Jack Lewis has described this stream of opposition as 'radical professionalism', which sees

> hierarchy and bureaucracy not as a by-product of the crisis in social expenditure but as the main problem in terms of the lack of democracy or not allowing 'qualified professionals' such as themselves to have a say in the policies of the department. For this current it is this lack of democracy within the state apparatus which is responsible for the other unpleasant aspects of social work. Such a perspective however leads to a struggle not on the side of the working class and against the capitalist state but on the contrary to a movement for improving and smoothing out the inner workings of the social services department.
>
> (Lewis, 1977, p. 123)

This conservative stream was evident in the settlement of the social workers' strike in 1979. To many who shared this perspective, the settlement which included the restructuring of the social worker's career system was warmly welcomed. Under this agreement, social services departments throughout the country began differentiating social workers into three bands. Each band was to be distinguished not only by salary levels but also by the kind of work considered to be appropriate. Thus field social workers selected for the highest level (number 3) were to be given considerable autonomy and allowed to concentrate on in-depth casework with selected clients, especially those such as children and problem families who were given high priority by the departments. Although level-3 social workers are expected to receive some supervision from line management on the whole they are expected to contribute to the supervision and 'development' of those social workers lower down the hierarchy.

This change in the career structure following the strike has in some important ways acted as an antidote to that persistent stream of professional discontent that characterised social services departments throughout the 1970s. Certainly, the more segmented and hierarchical division of labour which ensued was a most subtle form of labour management which has brought into social work employment a further set of self-disciplining forces. Professionally qualified social workers are aware that for some there is now a real possibility of being able to engage in the type of social work practice that is taught on the professional courses. But to reach this goal they also know that they will have to satisfy the social services management that they are loyal and capable workers trustworthy enough to be given the 'professional' freedoms that go with level-3 work. Thus for professionally qualified social workers there are some very pertinent rewards for keeping their heads down and not rocking the department.

RADICAL TRADE UNIONISM

Having pointed out that one stream within the growth of social worker trade unionism has been somewhat reluctant and in part conservative, there needs to be considered the new possibilities and opportunities that are emerging from the more political stream of social workers who are entering the trade-union movement.

One of the most significant of the early developments among socialist social workers was the magazine *Case Con*. Formed in the late 1960s this magazine constituted an important focus for the increasing number of radicals and socialists coming into social work. Apart from the regular publication of the journal, periodic meetings and gatherings were held of *Case Con* supporters, usually in London. These activities were valuable if only because they provided an important source of support for socialist and progressive workers who were often isolated in their work-places. Lots of issues were discussed, and critiques of social work orthodoxy and casework as well as professionalism were common themes. But by the mid-1970s the *Case Con* collective decided to stop the publication of the magazine and urged its supporters to direct their energies towards activities within the trade-union movement. This decision was important. It was not based on an idealistic view of the trade-union movement in general or NALGO in particular, and in the *Case Con Manifesto* (Bailey and Brake, 1975, pp. 144ff) it was made clear that socialist social workers would have to fight hard to achieve union democracy and to win over the union leadership to their political vision. In other words, the message from *Case Con* to its supporters was to join the union but with no illusions. This proviso remains crucial, particularly with respect to white-collar unions such as NALGO, where it is not uncommon to find a deeply entrenched conservative leadership who are extraordinarily well protected by the most elaborate sets of rules and organisational procedures which are capable of deflecting any attempt by socialists to move the union leftwards. In retrospect the decision of *Case Con* to advise workers to become active within their appropriate unions (NAPO, NALGO, NUPE) has proved fruitful. However, over recent years there has been a tendency to overstate this advice without warning of the possible pitfalls and dangers that come from directing one's energies in this way.

Corrigan and Leonard write that 'firstly and most importantly, it is essential that all social workers, and others in social welfare and community action, should join a trade union' (1978, p. 143). They also indicated that social workers may well find trade-union leaderships and bureaucracies unresponsive to their political demands, and argued that in order to prevent disillusionment social workers should recognise the limitations (on the revolutionary political front) and the strengths (power in bargaining on economistic issues) of the trade-union movement. Corrigan and Leonard then go on to argue that there are two possible Marxist strategies for working with the trade unions. One, which was recommended in the *Case Con Manifesto*, involves developing rank-and-file organisations within the established union structure. As they note, rank-and-file strategies are in part informed by the membership's critical stance towards the union leadership; indeed, Corrigan and Leonard argue, this policy involves 'encouraging the rank and file of the union to attack the leadership as a necessary first stage before the union can be mobilised on behalf of the true interest of the workers' (1978, p. 145).

For Corrigan and Leonard, however, the preferential strategy is to 'work within the institutions created by working class struggle over the past 100 years in spite of their imperfections and distortions'. For them, rank-and-file organisation is important, but not if it is directed solely towards attacking the union leadership; rather, its value lies in its capacity 'to utilise the strength of the organisations as a progressive force'.

Before criticising some of these points raised by Corrigan and Leonard we need to remember that their book was written before the social workers' strike of 1978—9. Thus their comments reflect their views on developments within the trade-union movement in general, and their concerns about the extent to which internecine struggles within unions between rank-and-file movements and union leaderships have weakened the unity and strength of the labour movement. They also reflect the many benefits which unionisation had brought to social workers in a vast array of small daily struggles, in which the evident power of the unions had protected and defended many individual social workers who had fallen foul of their managements.

One senses in their views a welcome sensitivity and concern about the possible reactions and legitimate caution of longstanding trade unionists suddenly confronted by a virulent rank-and-file movement of middle-class social workers who are not only white-collar state employees but also recent recruits to the organised labour movement.

Nevertheless, the manner in which the NALGO leadership, in particular, handled and co-ordinated the 1978—9 strike does throw into question Corrigan and Leonard's views about rank-and-file organisation and their preferred strategy of working more closely and co-operatively with the union leadership. For during the strike it became increasingly clear that some of the problems confronting the strikers were rooted in the conservatism of NALGO's leadership and organisation. This is not to say that white-collar unions such as NALGO are peculiarly conservative within the trade-union movement, for the evidence of the electricians' and plumbers' union under Frank Chapple and the engineers' under Terry Duffy demonstrates a far more vigorous conservatism than evidenced within NALGO. Nevertheless, white-collar unions such as NALGO do have a specific history and politics which has tended to inhibit radical trade unionism. A particular problem of such unions is that membershp is open to all grades of workers. Thus unions such as NALGO have members who occupy both senior management and also basic grade positions. Thus the union faces many problems when it comes to disputes within work-places where the opposing sides might both enjoy union membership and both can legitimately request union support. This clash of interest can often prevent union intervention. However, although NALGO is by no means a static union, and has moved a considerable distance from its early days at the beginning of this century when its General Secretary declared that 'anything savouring of trade unionism is nausea to the Local Government Officer and his Association' (cited in *Liverpool Strike News*, no. 7, 1978, p. 4), it remains the case that it is a union that can pose particular problems for progressive social workers. Thus, if progressive social workers are to be urged to join the union by groups such as *Case Con* and writers such as Corrigan and Leonard, then it is crucial that some of these problems are identified and recognised. For a failure to do so can lead to demoralisation and a paralysis of action.

WHITLEYISM

Many of these problems were highlighted during the 1978—9 social workers' strike. During that dispute many social worker activists were worried that they would be deserted by their union. Indeed, such was their anxiety that in November 1978, 600 social workers occupied their union headquarters in London for the purposes of preventing the union leadership from securing a 'solution' that did not meet their demands. This was just one of the many incidents which demonstrated fundamental differences between sections of the union leadership and the striking social workers, though, again, it should be noted that such clashes are not unique to NALGO.

At the root of many of these clashes was the union's adherence to the Whitley Council system of negotiation — a system which is common to most of the public-sector unions but which has been rejected by most of the powerful industrial unions. Whitleyism is a complex and fragmented system which consists of a series of joint councils at national, regional and local level. These councils are made up of equal numbers of employers and employees, and decisions can only be reached by a majority vote from *both* sides. The underlying spirit of Whitleyism is that of compromise in order to avoid industrial action. It is an extraordinarily drawn-out system of negotiation with unresolved compromises being shunted up and down the joint councils. Procedures for settling disputes within Whitleyism are rarely exhausted, so a union which dislikes strike action can usually find reasons for delaying industrial action by reference back to some new bureaucratic procedure.

Whitleyism directly confronted some of the major demands of the social workers. Many of the striking workers — and it must not be forgotten that the 1978—9 dispute was not a national strike of all social workers — were demanding a regrading of pay and conditions reflecting local conditions and commensurate with the increasing duties and responsibilities laid on them by social welfare legislation. One of the critical debates during the strike centred on the principle of local as against national negotiations for social workers' pay and conditions. In virtually every local authority affected by the strike, the majority feeling of the strikers was to go for local negotiations. This feeling became stronger as these social workers experienced the manner in which the union leadership manipulated the Whitley system and held out for national decisions and policies. It thus became clear to many militants that the only way that they would be able to achieve any significant influence over their work was to demand locally based negotiations that would dramatically shift the power away from the remote union bureaucrats to the rank-and-file members in the localities. This point was made clear in the *Liverpool Strike News*:

> Unless we can re-commit NALGO to local negotiations we will be back in the hands of our national negotiators, who will promptly sit on the issue as they have done in the past. Claims will not be drawn up, discussed and submitted and acted upon by the people whom they affect, but by professionals [non-social workers] . . . Local negotiations do not mean the end of Whitleyism . . . However, the nature of the social workers' struggle for local negotiations will severely weaken the system because the rank and file are involved. This is clearly easier at a local level than a national level, and is another reason why employers and NALGO bureaucrats (reared on Whitleyism) are anxious to scuttle the strikes.
>
> (*Strike News*, 15 January 1979, p. 4)

Although there were disagreements among the strikers about the issue of local negotiations, with some opposing this demand on the grounds supported by Corrigan and Leonard that it weakened the solidarity of the union and could lead less militant areas to suffer poor wages, in most of the strike areas the majority of the social workers involved became increasingly committed to the demand. And this commitment increased as the strike continued, for it became increasingly clear that the national leadership were anxious to end the strike on terms which were unfavourable to the social workers and were consistently attempting to undermine the strength of the rank and file.

While it is not possible to go into all the details of the social workers' strike — on which is difficult to generalise given that experiences varied from strike area to strike area — it did raise some important general issues concerning the nature of NALGO and demonstrated the need for social workers to become involved in developing effective grassroots activities within localities. Many of the gains which did result from the strike can be attributed to this form of action.

It was very often, for example, through such forms of organisation that social workers experienced for the first time the value of collective action and strength. By refusing to allow the officers of NALGO to run the dispute through the confusing channels of Whitley Councils, rank-and-file members were able to make some valuable alliances with sections of the working class, particularly those who had long experiences of industrial disputes such as local authority and public service manual workers, and, in areas such as Merseyside, with car workers. Indeed, it was often the case that social workers gained more support — moral and financial — from this section of the labour movement than they did from other sections of their own union working within local government. These new contacts were important, for they allowed social workers to talk with other workers, face to face, not only about the specifics of their strike, but also about the problems and issues of social welfare policies in general. In some areas the organised labour movement was able to gain new insights into the nature of the personal social services. This in turn led to more detailed discussions about the manner in which certain positive *service* aspects of the personal social services were being eroded through the cuts in public spending. Similarly, through these direct links, the standing of many social workers rose in the eyes of working-class activists and the possibilities for more firm alliances between middle-class state employees and the manual and semi-skilled working class in the long-established industrial unions were enhanced.

While the strike did expose weaknesses within the union's structure and politics, at all levels, and inevitably exposed social workers' inexperience in organising industrial action, it was nevertheless an important moment in social work's history, and the repercussions will undoubtedly ripple on for some time. Simpkin, for example, in his second edition of *Trapped Within Welfare* (1983) has noted the rapid politicisation of many of those who took part in the strike in Sheffield, of the ways in which new and creative relationships were forged, and new skills and confidences uncovered, with consequences which have endured the subsequent settlement. Undoubtedly some of the gains made at that time, especially those generated on the picket-lines, have subsequently faltered in the period since the strike, but there can be no return to that period when the very idea of trade unionism in social welfare work was thought to be almost a contradiction in terms, and neither is there any reason to suppose that trade unionism will not continue to flourish and develop with social workers making further contributions to the organised labour movement.

This important episode in the development of social work reinforced the need for social workers to continue in their efforts to develop rank-and-file organisations within unions such as NALGO. While Corrigan and Leonard's concern about the divisive consequences of some forms of rank-and-file organisation on the unity of the trade-union movement is understandable, the particular characteristics of NALGO were seen to require such initiatives. In common with other white-collar unions, it is not always clear whether NALGO regards itself as an association of managers and professionals or as a fully fledged trade union committed to advancing the interests of all those who are compelled to sell their labour-power in order to survive. A militant rank and file within NALGO which united workers throughout local government could do much to develop this now major trade union, and to ensure its contribution to the formulation of progressive policies within the organised labour movement as a whole.

ORGANISING: SENSITIVITY AND IMAGINATION

Nevertheless while there are many advantages to working within the institutions of the organised labour movement, other form and possible areas of action should not be ruled out. After all, working within some union branches can be unrewarding and a drain on energies and commitment. Some union branches have entrenched leaderships well able to manipulate intricate and mystifying organisational procedures to secure their power base and protect them from militant opposition. For those activists who enjoy the support of a good union branch it is all too easy to recommend union

involvement as the main site of social worker activism and to
be dismissive of other strategies. Some social workers do lack
a supportive union branch that welcomes and encourages
their participation. Imagination is needed in helping to create
campaigns which bring together all those committed to
fundamental and radical social change.

Such sensitivity is necessary irrespective of the relative
merits of any union branch in which social workers are
members given that so many clients are outside of the organised
labour movement either because of age, handicap and,
increasingly, unemployment. Social workers can and should
attempt to bridge and reconcile some of the differences that
have divided the working class, and in particular to extend
the politics of organised labour to include the marginal and
residual poor. These tasks require considerable thought and
imagination which is not assisted by rigid assumptions
narrowly delineating areas and sites of struggle.

In the development of social workers' politics, therefore,
we should be alert to the implications of an impressively wide
array of campaigns and activities which have included social
workers. Unfortunately, in Britain at least, little record has
been preserved of campaigns for a more humane society
when they are neither of national significance nor located
within the recognised organisations of the labour movement.
Yet it has often been within this 'hidden' history and tradition of working-class struggle that social workers have been
most active and from which arise some practical opportunities
for progressive social workers to contribute to the development of a more unified working class response to particular
problems and issues.

The Action on Debt group in Northern Ireland provides a
fine example of the value of social workers becoming involved in a broad alliance of community and labour organisations. AOD was initially established by the women's movement in Ulster in response to large-scale fuel poverty and
debt in the province. It subsequently expanded to include
social workers (BASW in Ulster supported the campaign),
trade unionists, including those from the fuel industries, and
claimants and others who suffer fuel problems. In 1981 AOD
published a pamphlet entitled *Sticking the Knife In*, a power-

ful critique of the British state's fuel and energy policy and a most inspiring testament to the political potential and advantage that can flow from a diverse group of people coming together.

In this campaign social workers have been able to make a contribution to a fuel campaign which is firmly rooted within a socialist politics. Moreover, by drawing upon the experiences of those employed in the fuel industries, those charged by the state to manage the consequences such as social workers and social security officials, and not least those for whom debt is such a problem, AOD was able to move beyond a solitary focus on welfare rights to a wider assessment of the inequalities of capitalist economies and social policies. Their pamphlet offers considerable insights to progressive social workers and provides a practical and realistic example of what can be achieved in campaigns of this sort. It is especially relevant that this campaign actively confronted the populist myths so often encouraged in the media that most debtors are the irresponsible, idle and scrounging poor, and demonstrates the political potential which flourishes once it is accepted that debt is not a symptom of personal failure but rather of inadequate resources and a powerlessness to affect decisions — a powerlessness which characterises and threatens the lives of all working people, albeit in varying degrees of intensity.

CONSIDERING ALTERNATIVES: THE COERCIVE TILT

Just as many social workers are becoming increasingly aware of the need to become involved in a wide variety of campaigns and in trade-union work, so they should consider more carefully and energetically possible visions of what social welfare policy could be, and in turn be more precise about the strategies and policies that should be developed within, say, the Labour party and the TUC. This aspect of socialist politics has moved increasingly into focus as the restructuring of the state has gathered momentum. Walker and Beaumont (1981) have described as a 'coercive tilt' the movement whereby the state apparatus becomes more authoritarian and punitive in its attempts to restore social order and strips away rights and access to welfare services on the grounds that such policies through their burden on expenditure and effect on social morality have been signficant factors in the recurrent economic crises of British capitalism.

For at least the last ten years social workers have directly experienced in their agencies this gradual but accelerating shift towards a more coercive state system. In material terms they have seen their ability to provide services substantially curtailed; they have witnessed marked reductions in the availability of residential provision and yet a corresponding increase in the organisational and bureaucratic checks and controls over their work. Related and concomitant changes in other areas of state policy have also accelerated the process of coercive tilt within the personal social services, a most notable example being the 1980 Social Security Acts (Novak, 1981). The therapeutic casework orientation of social work is no longer the guiding principle of local authority social work. Rather, social work now owes its persistence and survival not so much to its claims to rehabilitate to citizenship the marginal and deviant poor but to its capacity to service smoothly the primary welfare agencies, to ration resources, and above all, as Pinker recognised, to 'contain crises . . . and trying to prevent matters from getting worse' (1979, p. 596). It is no surprise to see, therefore, in the findings of the Barclay Working Party a general support for social work precisely on the grounds that it performs these 'indispensable' tasks (Barclay, 1982, pp. 123–5). This perspective is also reflected in the Working Party's acceptance that social workers 'carry the burden of failures in social policy' (p. 45) and that social workers are particularly useful as rationers and gatekeepers of scare resources because they are sympathetic and humane! (pp. 46–7).

An example of the implications of this process of 'coercive tilt' for social work practice was given by some Manchester probation officers:

Recent policy formation in Greater Manchester aroused strong feelings amongst NAPO members because it seemed to involve a fundamental change in our work; from being primarily of a social work nature to being primarily of a surveillance nature, involving the containment of high risk offenders. Along with this was to be a substantial reduction in officer autonomy, and a move towards management by autocratic direction, rather than by consultation.

(Adam *et al.*, 1980, p. 118)

It is again worth noting that the Barclay Working Party also argued that 'surveillance' was now a key component of contemporary social work practice (Barclay, 1982, p. 12).

UNDERSTANDING CAPITALISM

These fundamental shifts in the nature of social work which are taking it increasingly away from its post-1945 social democractic roots are pressing social workers of all political opinions to consider alternatives. Clearly for some the emergence of the Social Democratic Party holds out hope, particularly those who ascribe to the traditional professional objectives of social work and find in the SDP support for that policy and a belief in the legitimacy of professional experts and their need for some autonomy. It would therefore seem likely that the SDP, with its commitment to the 'consensus politics' of the post-war era and a welfare state structure, not the least one suspects because of the many benefits it brought to the liberal middle classes in terms of lucrative careers and enhanced status, will attract the support of those social workers whom Lewis described as 'radical professionals'.

For many socialists, however, the policies of the SDP and radical professionalism provide no alternative. Indeed, any attempt to turn back the clock and to unpick the various shifts to the right could never be successful given that the restructuring of the British state is but just one aspect of fundamental developments within the international system of capital. The locus of power does not rest solely in Whitehall, and nation-states are having to dance increasingly to the tunes of the large transnational corporations and the power of international capital.

Already, many of the world's leading multinationals have served notice on those nation-states that continue to govern in accordance with the dictates of liberal social democracy that they will shift their productive bases to those areas of the developing world that can guarantee cheap and disciplined labour, that control and preferably prohibit trade unions, that do not impose taxes and duties on industrial activities in order to finance rising government expenditure, and that do not operate health and safety procedures that inhibit the exploitation of labour (Bodington, 1982, ch. 1). Similarly Navarro (1982) has shown how international capital confronted with its most profound crisis has sought to restructure 'welfare states' throughout the core capitalist states within the western world with the intent of undermining the power of the working class, to lower dramatically people's expectations, to encourage a new spirit of individualistic self-help and to reduce social expenditure.

Although it is not unexpected that large sections of the parliamentary Conservative, Labour, Liberal and Social Democratic parties have not fully come to terms with the maturing power of transnational capital, it is concerning that so few socialists have confronted this situation. For, as Bodington argues, oppositional work and debates about strategy and alternatives must be based on an accurate understanding of modern capitalism in its contemporary stage of transnationalised capitalism: 'Few socialists', he observes, 'have really addressed themselves to the reality of the changes that have been going on in the world; too many have played with theoretical models of the past like boys with tin soldiers from the Crimean War' (1982, p. 34).

Thus while the issues surrounding this phase of transnationalised capital may seem theoretically and even geographically remote from the debates and struggles surrounding social work and clients, its impact is nevertheless influential and must be considered. Even at this early stage it would seem safe to conclude that the onslaught on the working classes in the western 'core' countries will continue and that welfare states will similarly slide further along the coercive tilt. For social work specifically it would seem likely that the current pattern of development with its emphasis on crisis management, servicing, rationing and surveillance will continue. This was certainly the principal thrust of the Barclay Working Party, which in time may come to be viewed as one of the key documents which signals the final end of the expansive, holistic and naively ambitious era of social work encompassed in the 1969 Children and Young Persons Act and the 1968 Seebohm Report. Barclay does, however, acknowledge that this shift is causing problems and notes, for example, the relationship between bureaucratisation and unionisation (1982, p. 180). Similarly, the Working Party recognised that social workers were becoming increasingly resentful about the manner in which their jobs now involved more rationing and social policing work, and managing the inadequacies of other institutions and government policies (pp. 109—10). The Working Party suggested that organisational structures should be modified to allow social workers to express their views and that local councils should not expect their social workers to 'accept things as they are and work silently with individuals and families' (p. 110). While these sentiments would appear laudable two qualifications are necessary which would suggest significantly different sentiments. First, the Working Party was aware that the credibility of social workers in the eyes of their clients depends in part on them not being viewed 'as unquestioning servants of what is regarded as a hostile authority', and second, close limits are placed on the extent of social workers' opposition:

> We recognise that, in the last resort, social workers, like other local authority employees, have to accept the decisions the authority takes or, if they see an unsupportable conflict between their clients' interests and the authority's policy, to move to other jobs.
>
> (Barclay Report, 1982, p. 111)

SOCIAL DEMOCRACY IN RETREAT

But perhaps like most working party reports the most pertinent clues to Barclay's significance lie as much in what is not said as in what is. Those who have followed the professional literature of the last decade, or studied the extensive research findings of the DHSS-funded investigation of social services departments (Parsloe *et al.*, 1978), will find in the Barclay Report none of the outrage, disappointment or anxieties which featured highly in those publications. There is no grieving in Barclay about the lack of opportunity in contemporary social services departments to undertake intensive and supposedly therapeutic work with clients, there is no outrage about dwindling resources and growing client need, and no doubts about rationing and surveillance work. These omissions support the argument that the nature of current state social work has to be considered differently: that we can no longer proceed as though social democracy was still the decisive influence. This is a different position from that taken by Bolger *et al.* (1981) in *Towards Socialist Welfare Work*. As the authors note, the persistence of the social democratic influence has a special significance for their analysis and for their prescriptions for practice:

> We feel it is possible to argue for this form of movement towards socialist welfare work because we are discussing *social democratic state apparatuses*. Even given the present policy of the Conservative Party we do not feel that it will be possible to shift welfare state structures from within that social democratic framework for a considerable period of time. It is true that governments may try to do so and in fact make enormous inroads, but social democracy does have a real power over the hearts and minds of working people.
>
> (Bolger *et al.*, 1981, p. 147)

While not disputing their arguments concerning the influence of social democracy upon the development of state social work since 1945, it is now questionable whether social services departments can be described as social democratic state institutions in any meaningful sense. Moreover, persisting with such a view is asking social work practitioners to work on contradictions which were once a significant feature of social democratic institutions but which are no longer important. In the few years since *Towards Socialist Welfare Work* was written there have been further major retreats from the influence of social democracy with fundamental consequences for the state agencies which were shaped under its aegis. Indeed, the purposes underlying the restructuring of the welfare state have been to curtail dramatically the progressive features of welfare policy: to restrict rights, to limit services, to make allocation more difficult and stigmatising. In turn, employing authorities have taken an overall tougher stance with social workers, instigating new contracts of employment, using the threat of dismissal or redundancy, manipulating extended career structures to secure tranquillity and using powers such as secondment for training as a reward for conformity. Undoubtedly there are other processes at work which (implicitly or explicitly) attempt to achieve the same goals.

Developments such as these are moving social work away from its recent social democratic foundations towards it becoming little more than an emergency ambulance service with more abrasive and restrictive criteria as to whom it assists, and how. Moreover, it is a movement which encompasses the welfare state system as a whole. Thus whereas the work of Corrigan and Leonard (1978) was insightful in drawing attention to the 'inevitable' contradictions of social democracy and its institutions, and the possibilities it allowed for progressive practice, there is now a markedly changed state formation with different contradictions requiring new and different responses.

IMMEDIATE AND MEDIUM-TERM STRATEGIES

This book has attempted to outline realistic strategies which can be undertaken by progressive social workers. Given the changes which are taking place in the state and in political ideology, it would seem particularly important that socialists in social work should do their utmost to maintain a broad front of oppositional work. As Walker and Beaumont have argued: 'In a period of coercive tilt, an oppositional stance will be particularly important: changes in the job will need to be resisted and opportunities for progressive development are likely to be limited'. (1981, p. 169).

Such oppositional work can take a wide variety of forms, and social workers will be selecting those forms that are most suited to their particular situation and the levels of support they can expect in their work-places. Without doubt, given the coercive tilt and the shift towards tougher managerial systems within many local authorities, social workers are having to pay greater attention to the manner in which they undertake such work. Managing one's appearances, taking care in how issues are raised, seeking out and winning support, are all now necessary tactics. Thus, while the opportunities on the job for developing new progressive initiatives are now limited, there still remains many opportunities to continue low-level but important oppositional strategies. These may include defending clients against some aspects of the criminal justice system through the preparation of social enquiry reports which minimise the use of custodial sentences; early recommendations for relinquishing supervision orders on juvenile offenders which can be of great value if the youngster re-offends; pressing for resources for clients; working alongside clients to modify the decisions of the many statutory bodies with which they have contact; and not least being aware of the non-statutory resources in work areas (e.g. unemployed workers' unions, women's groups) which can often help clients in a more positive and meaningful way.

High priority must be given to exposure work. Social work is a sensitive area of activity for the state and the ruling class. It is the domain of casualties who expose the frailties and brutalities of a capitalist society. The state pays considerable attention and makes strenuous efforts to disguise this domain; to keep the problems hidden from general view and to promote explanations which transfer responsibility to the victims themselves. This *cordon sanitaire* has many implications for working-class politics, not least in separating large clusters of the residual and deviant poor from the rest of the working population, and removing and obfuscating a vital source of potential anger. All indicators at the moment, including the report of the Barclay Working Party, point to these activities being stepped up as the recession and cuts bite deeper into the life-chances and circumstances of the poor. The DHSS may turn out to be even more vigilant in its control over sensitive and embarrassing data. Already a doctor has alleged manipulation of death certificates in order to disguise the number of fatalities due to hypothermia (*Bulletin on Social Policy* no. 8, 1981, p. 21), and it would be surprising if the DHSS has not made plans to prevent a repeat of the Black Report (1980), which through using official sources embarrassed the government by demonstrating that class inequalities in health had not narrowed since the introduction of the National Health Service, and in some instances had widened.

It is this sensitivity which progressive social workers should work on and use their considerable experience of and contact with clients to expose their appalling and deteriorating plight. This contact is potentially one of the most important features available for progressive exploitation by social workers. This book's historical overview of social work's development has demonstrated that it was this theme which in the main influenced the training, education, selection and organisation of social workers. Moreover, these controls are increasing. However, while some social workers have engaged in 'whistle-blowing' activities, it has not been extensive, nor has the Left given a great deal of consideration to the ways in which it can be undertaken. These discussions must be started, and extra care must be taken in cataloguing and listing those organisations, resource and socialist centres, trade unions and councils, publications, etc. that would be willing to use the insights and information provided. In some respects a *State Research* equivalent for the welfare state could be a useful starting-point. Social workers can make a valuable contribution to the class struggle; but as yet, however, only occasional glimpses of the potential of that contribution have been witnessed. In many respects the key could well be the extent to which social workers can help create a union structure that will provide the necessary organisational means and political strength that will allow them to report on their experiences amidst the working-class poor and from within the state without fear of victimisation. Clearly, if a way cannot be found to use 'whistle-blowing' material effectively and in a way which does not jeopardise the 'whistle-blower' then the strategy will never develop.

Apart from these immediate and day-to-day oppositional activities, longer-term policies ought to be considered. In particular, a question that seems especially relevant in the medium term concerns the policies to be ennacted and pursued should a left-wing Labour government come to power. No attempt is made here to develop a blue-print, but rather this question needs attention and social workers should consider their responses. Important sections of the Labour party have at last recognised that a radical alternative is required both to the Conservative party's monetarist and restrictive state policies and to its own brand of reformist social democracy. As a result the Labour party has experienced a wave of intensive theoretical activity with leading party intellectuals drawing up ideas and plans (Cripps *et al.*, 1981).

Already a major theme concerning democratisation of state institutions and services is emerging from these discussions (Bolger *et al.*, 1981; Griffiths, 1982). This demand arises largely from the growing recognition that many of the welfare services created under social democracy concentrated powers in the hands of unaccountable 'professional experts' — which was a key reason why so many of the working-class consumers of such services found them to be patronising and stigmatising. These demands are important, and raise central questions about power and interests in the control of welfare which social workers need to confront.

But, as Simpkin (1983, ch. 8) has warned, we need to be wary of the problems associated with the democratisation strategy. Given the absence of a vibrant mass socialist movement in Britain one cannot be sure that democratisation will lead to the improvement in welfare services needed. With respect to social work there are within working-class culture long-standing antagonistic strands towards some clusters of the client population. It would not be in the interests of clients to find under democratisation that power had shifted away from unaccountable experts and administrators to the representatives of the 'moral majority'.

Although the strategy of democratisation does pose

difficult problems, there are other levels at which the concept has more immediate value for social welfare workers. Many residential homes — an area which has been neglected — are particularly appropriate areas in which power should be transferred to the residents. In many homes this decision would very rapidly eradicate any tendency towards institutionalisation, and in the longer term such democratised welfare provision could offer valuable indicators to viable alternatives to the family institution.

Crucial to all these discussions is information: the extent of unmet or partially met need; the ways in which current services are inadequate in material terms; the ways in which the services transmit stigmatising ideologies; social audits of all kinds should be undertaken assessing the impact and interlationship of services; and not least, social workers should be talking to and listening with clients. The Leeds Social Work Action Group has been engaged in some of these activities and one would suspect that their gathering of information was also an important politicising activity as workers and clients considered the shortfalls in provision and, in the case of Leeds, observed that their city was well down the league of services provided in comparative cities. Coupled with public meetings and discussions the publication of these 'audits' expose deficiencies and also open up previously restricted areas.

Thus there are many possibilities. As always the problem is in deciding where and how energies should be used to best effect, and I hope that this book's analysis provides some useful indicators. Above all, a clear and hard-headed perspective needs to be maintained. Social work, within its radical and established traditions, has often shown a tendency towards grandiosity, which at times has led social workers to neglect the value of important low-level oppositional and defensive work, and to ignore the necessity of seeking out those parts from the daily practice of state social work which offer concrete and realistic progressive opportunities. It is also important that the changes in the state are recognised; as social democracy retreats, there exists a more hostile work environment, reinforced by the successes of abrasive management techniques used with such effect in the steel, motor-car and railway industries. To ignore these new constraints and to neglect building up strategies of self-defence would be folly. But, on the other hand, as the recession and public expenditure cuts exert their toll so new tensions and problems will arise for the state. It seems probable that state social work will continue to be used and developed as a major strategy for controlling some of these conflicts, and given its contradictory character social work will continue to be a site of considerable argument and controversy with risks to the state and renewed possibilities for socialists.

Bibliography

Action on Debt (1981) *Sticking the Knife In: Debt and Debt Collection in Northern Ireland*, AOD, Belfast.

Adams S., Moss L. and Pleasance, G. (1980) 'Who Makes Policy: Why and How?', *Probation Journal*, vol. 27, December.

Alden, P. (1905) *The Unemployed: A National Question*, P. S. King, London.

Anon. (1968) 'Social Values and Social Work in the UK' mimeo report, Joint University Council for Social and Public Administration, London.

Armitage, R. (1968) 'Content and Method of Training', *British Hospital Journal and Social Service Review*, vol. LXXVII (4079).

Association of Community Workers (1982) *Successes and Struggles on Council Estates*, ACW, London.

Association of Social Workers (1959) *Morals and the Social Worker*, Report of Conference, St Edmund Hall, Oxford.

Bailey, R. and Brake, M. (ed.) (1975) *Radical Social Work*, Edward Arnold, London.

Bailey, R. and Brake, M. (1975a) 'Social Work in the Welfare State', in Bailey and Brake (1975).

Baker, J. (1979) 'Social Conscience and Social Policy', *Journal of Social Policy*, vol. 8(2).

Barclay Working Party Report (1982) *Social Workers: Their Role and Tasks*, National Institute for Social Work/National Council of Voluntary Organisations, London.

Beaumont, B. (1976) 'A Supportive Role', *Probation Journal*, vol. 23(3).

Beloff, M. (1979) *The State and its Servants*, Conservative Political Centre, London.

Beresford, P. and Beresford, S. (1980—1) *Community Control of Social Service Departments*, Battersea Community Action, London.

Bernstein, S. (1960) 'Self-Determination: King or Citizen in the Realm of Values?', *Social Work* (US), January, pp. 3—8.

Biestek, F. P. (1954) 'An Analysis of the Casework Relationship', *Social Casework*, vol. 35(2).

Birmingham Children's Defence Campaign (1979) *In Defence of Children*, BCDC, Birmingham.

Black Report (1980) *Report of the Working Group on Inequalities in Health*, DHSS, London.

Bodington, S. (1982) *The Cutting Edge of Socialism: Working People against Transnational Capital*, Spokesman Books, Nottingham.

Bolger, S., Corrigan, P., Docking, J., and Frost, N. (1981) *Towards Socialist Welfare Work*, Macmillan, London.

Bosanquet, B. (1890) 'The Antithesis between Individualism and Socialism', *Charity Organisation Review*, September, pp. 357—68.

Bosanquet, B. (1893) *The Civilisation of Christendom*, Swan Sonnenschein, London.

Bosanquet, B. (ed.) (1895) *Aspects of the Social Problem*, Macmillan, London.

Bosanquet, B. (1898) 'Idealism in Social Work', *Charity Organisation Review*, vol. 3, pp. 122—33.

Bosanquet, B. (1901) 'Meaning of Social Work', *International Journal of Ethics*, vol. 11.

Bosanquet, B. (1915) 'Politics and Charity', *Charity Organisation Review*, vol. 38.

Bosanquet, B. (1916) 'The Philosophy of Casework', *Charity Organisation Review*, vol. 39.

Bosanquet, H. (1893) 'The Industrial Residuum', *Economic Journal*, vol. 3.

Bosanquet, H. (1900) 'Methods of Training', *Charity Organisation Review*, August.

Bosanquet, H. (1902) *The Strength of the People*, Macmillan, London.

Bosanquet, H. (1906) *The Family*, Macmillan, London.

Bosanquet, H. (1914) *Social Work in London 1869—1912*, John Murray, London.

Bowlby, J. (1953) *Child Care and the Growth of Love*, Penguin, Harmondsworth.

Brandon, D. (1975) 'Clients have a Right to Hope for Better Privacy Than This', *Community Care*, 23 April.

Brandon, J. and Davies, M. (1979) 'The Limits of Competence in Social Work: The Assessment of Marginal Students in Social Work Education', *British Journal of Social Work*, vol. 9(3).

Braverman, H. (1974) *Labour and Monopoly Capital*, Monthly Review Press, New York.

Brewer, C. and Lait, J. (1980) *Can Social Work Survive?*, Temple Smith, London.

Bristol BMA (1959) *Report of the Joint Committee of the Bristol Division of the BMA and the Bristol Local Medical Committee on the Prevention of the Break Up of Families*, BMA, Bristol.

British Association of Social Workers (1973) *The Inalienable Element in Social Work*, BASW, Birmingham.

Brown, M. and Foren, R. (1970) *An Analysis of Promotion Patterns in the Probation Service in England and Wales*, NAPO, London.

Bryant, M., Coker, J. *et al.* (1978) 'Sentenced to Social Work', *Probation Journal*, vol. 25(4).

Buckingham, G., Dimmock, B. and Trustcott, D. (1979) *Beyond Tea, Bingo and Condescension*, Beth Johnson Foundation/Task Force, London.

Byrne, D. (1973) *Problem Families: A Lumpen-Proletariat*, Working Papers in Sociology No. 5, Durham University.

Carmichael, K. (1976) 'Freud: Explorer of the Inner Life', *Community Care*, 18 August.

Carr Saunders, A. M., Mannheim, H. and Rhodes, E. C. (1943) *Young Offenders*, Cambridge University Press, Cambridge.

Central Council for Education and Training in Social Work (1975) *Education and Training for Social Work*, CCETSW Discussion Paper No. 10.

Centre for Contemporary Cultural Studies (Education Group) (1981) *Unpopular Education*, Hutchinson, London.

Coates, K. and Silburn, R. (1970) *Poverty: The Forgotten Englishman*, Penguin, Harmondsworth.

Collins, D. (1965) 'The Introduction of Old Age Pensions in GB', *Historical Journal*, vol. 8(2).

Corner, E. P. (1959) Untitled contribution in Association of Social Workers (1959).

Corrigan, Philip (1977) 'State Formation and Moral Regulation in 19th Century Britain', unpublished Ph.D. thesis, University of Durham.

Corrigan, Philip (ed.) (1980) *Capitalism, State Formation and Marxist Theory*, Quartet, London.

Corrigan, Philip and Corrigan, V. (1979) 'State Formation and Social Policy until 1871', in Parry *et al.* (1979).

Corrigan, Philip and Gilespie, V. (1978) *Class Struggle, Social Literacy and Idle Time*, Labour History Monographs, Brighton.

Corrigan, Paul (1977) 'The Welfare State as an Arena of Class Struggle', *Marxism Today*, March.

Corrigan, Paul and Leonard, Peter (1978) *Social Work Practice Under Capitalism*, Macmillan, London.

Council for Training in Social Work (1967) *Third Report*, CTSW, London.

Council for Training in Social Work (1971) *The Teaching of Fieldwork*, Discussion Paper No. 4, CTSW, London.

Coventry, Liverpool, Newcastle, North Tyneside Trades Councils (1980) *State Intervention in Industry: A Worker's Enquiry*, Trades Council, Newcastle upon Tyne.

Cowley, J. (1977) 'The Politics of Community Organising', in Cowley *et al.* (1977).

Cowley, J., Kaye, A., Mayo, M. and Thompson, M. (eds) (1977) *Community or Class Struggle*, Stage 1, London.

Cripps, F. *et al.* (1981) *Manifesto: A Radical Strategy for Britain's Future*, Pan Books, London.

Crosland, A. (1956) *The Future of Socialism*, Jonathan Cape, London.

Curtis Committee (1946) *Report of the Care of Children Committee*, Cmnd 6922, HMSO, London.

Cypher, J. (1979) 'Social Work Training: Davies Rocks the BASW Boat', *Community Care*, 6 December.

Davies, B. (1980) 'Policies and Priorities in Youth and Community Work: A Review of Two Decades', in F. Booton and A. Dearling (eds), *The 1980s and Beyond*, National Youth Bureau, Leicester.

Davies, B. (1981) *The State We're In*, National Youth Bureau, Leicester.

Davies, M. (1981) *The Essential Social Worker*, Tavistock, London.

Davies, M. (1981a) 'What We Have to Learn about Social Work Education', *Community Care*, 15 January.

Davis, K. (1938) 'Mental Hygiene and the Class Structure', *Psychiatry*, vol. 1, February.

Department of Education and Science (1964) *Education under Social Handicap*, Reports on Education No. 17, HMSO, London.

Donnison, D. (1928) 'Seebohm: The Report and its Implications', *Social Work* (UK), October.

Donzelot, J. (1979) *The Policing of Families*, Hutchinson, London.

Engels, F. (1973) *The Condition of the Working Class in England*, Lawrence & Wishart, London.

Ensor, R. C. K. (1950) 'The Problem of Quantity and Quality in the British Population', *Eugenics Review*, vol. 13(3).

Equal Opportunities Commission (1980) *The Experience of Caring for Elderly and Handicapped Dependents*, EOC, Manchester.

Gallacher, W. (1951) *Rise Like Lions*, Lawrence & Wishart, London.

Gardiner, R. K. and Judd, H. O. (1959) *The Development of Social Administration*, Oxford University Press, Oxford.

Garrett, A. (1949) 'Historical Survey of the Evolution of Casework', *Journal of Social Casework*, vol. 30(6).

Gettleman, M. E. (1974) 'The Whig Interpretation of Social Welfare History', *Smith College Studies in Social Work*, vol. XLIV, June.

Gilbert, P. (1979) 'Socking the Social Services', *Community Care*, 1 February.

Ginsburg, N. (1979) *Class, Capital and Social Policy*, Macmillan, London.

Goldberg, E. M. *et al.* (1970) *Helping the Aged*, Allen & Unwin, London.

Goldberg, E. M. (1974) 'Dilemmas in Social Work', *Journal of Psychosomatic Research*, vol. 18.

Gould, J. (1977) *The Attack on Higher Education: Marxism and Radical Penetration*, Institute for the Study of Conflict, London.

Gow, H. J. (1900) 'Methods of Training II', *Charity Organisation Review*, vol. 8.

Griffiths, D. (1982) 'The Responsiveness of Local Services', *Bulletin on Social Policy*, no. 11, summer.

Hadley, R. and McGrath, M. (1979) 'Patch Based Social Services', *Community Care*, 11 October.

Haines, J. (1967) 'Satisfaction in Social Work', *New Society*, 5 January.

Handler, J. F. (1968) 'The Coercive Children's Officer', *New Society*, 3 October.

Harris, J. (1972) *Unemployment and Politics*, Clarendon Press, Oxford.

Health Ministry (1954) *Break Up of Families and Health of Children*, Circular 27/54, printed in the *Medical Officer*, 10 December 1954.

Health and Social Security Department (1976) *Priorities For the Health and Personal Social Services*, HMSO, London.

Heraud, B. J. (1967) 'Teaching of Sociology in Professional Social Work Courses', unpublished paper given to the Sociology Teachers Section of the BSA conference.

Heraud, B. J. (1970) *Sociology and Social Work*, Pergamon Press, Oxford.

Heraud, B. J. (1972) 'Professionalisation in Social Work', unpublished Ph.D. thesis, University of London.

Heywood, J. (1964) *An Introduction to Teaching Casework Skills*, Routledge & Kegan Paul, London.

Hill, M. (1969) 'The Exercise of Discretion in the National Assistance Board', *Public Administration*, Spring.

Hill, O. (1884) *Homes of the London Poor*, Macmillan, London.

Holman, H. (1914) 'Training for Secretaries', *Charity Organisation Review*, vol. 36.

Home Office (with the Ministry of Education) (1949) *Memorandum on Juvenile Delinquency*, HMSO, London.

Home Office (1951) *The Sixth Report on the Work of the Children's Department*, HMSO, London.

Howarth, E. (1953) 'Definition and Diagnosis of the Social Problem Family', *Social Work* (UK), vol. 10(1).

Hutchins, P. L. (1913) *Conflicting Ideals: Two Sides of the Woman's Question*, P. Murby, London.

Irvine, E. E. (1954) 'Research into Problem Families', *British Journal of Psychiatric Social Work*, vol. 9, Spring.

Jeffrys, M. (1965) *An Anatomy of Social Welfare Services*, Michael Joseph, London.

Johnson, R. (1980) 'Education and Social Democracy', *Socialism and Education*, vol. 5(5).

Jones, C. (1976) *The Foundations of Social Work Education*, Working Papers in Sociology No. 11, University of Durham.

Jones, C. (1978) 'An Analysis of the Development of Social Work and Social Work Education 1869–1977', unpublished Ph.D. thesis, University of Durham.

Jones, C. (1979) 'Social Work Education 1900–1977', in Parry *et al.* (1979).

Jones, C. (1981) 'The Computerisation of Social Service Departments', *Bulletin on Social Policy*, no. 8.

Jones, C. and Novak, T. (1980) 'The State and Social Policy', in Corrigan (1980).

Jones, D. (1950) untitled paper on problem families in Salford (1950).

Jordan, B. (1981) 'A Platform Creaking', *Social Work Today*, 22 September.

Kahan, B. (1968) 'Child Care and Social Services Departments', *Social Work* (UK), vol. 25(4).

Kahn, A. J. (1970) 'Social Work and the Control of Delinquency', in Lerman (1970).

Karpf, M. J. (1931) *The Scientific Basis of Social Work*, Columbia University Press, New York.

Kendall, K. A. (1972) 'Dream or Nightmare? The Future of Social Work Education', *Social Work Today*, vol. 3(16).

Kirkman Gray, B. (1908) *Philanthropy and the State*, P. S. King, London.

Kitchen, M. (1980) 'What the Client Thinks of You', *Social Work Today*, 3 June.

Kuhn, T. S. (1962) *The Structure of Scientific Revolutions*, University of Chicago Press, Chicago.

Lamont, A. (1981) 'Social Workers: A Soft Touch for Spongers?', *Social Work Today*, 3 March.

Lang, T. and Castledine, E. (1979) 'Social Work is Not Enough', *Bulletin on Social Policy*, no. 4, Autumn.

Lawrance, M. (1950) untitled paper in Salford (1950).

Leach, S. N. (1981) 'Relationships between Supplementary Benefits Offices and Social Service Departments', *Policy and Politics*, vol. 9(3).

Lee, W. E. (1973) 'Conflict of Model', *New Society*, 23 August.

Leonard, P. (1966) *Sociology in Social Work*, Routledge & Kegan Paul, London.

Leonard, P. (1968) 'Social Policy and Social Work', *Medical Social Work*, vol. 20(9).

Leonard, P. (1973) 'Professionalisation, Community Action and the Growth of Social Service Bureaucracies', in *Sociological Review Monograph*, no. 20, ed. P. Halmos.

Leonard, P. (1976) 'The Function of Social Work in Society', in Timms and Watson (1976).

Leonard, P. (1979) 'Restructuring the Welfare State', *Marxism Today*, December.

Lerman, P. (ed.) (1970) *Delinquency and Social Policy*, Praeger, New York.

Lewis, J. (1977) 'British Capitalism, the Welfare State and the First Radicalisation of State Employees, in Cowley *et al.* (1977).

Liddiard, R. and Paynter, B. (1978) 'Education and Training Balance is Questionable', *Social Work Today* 11 May.

Loch, C. S. (1904) *Methods of Social Advance*, Macmillan, London.

Loch, C. S. (1906) *Introduction to Annual Charities Register and Digest*, 15 edn, Longman, London.

Loch, C. S. (1923) *A Great Ideal and its Champion*, London, Allen & Unwin.

London—Edinburgh Weekend Return Group (1979) *In and Against the State*, CSE, London.

McDougall, M. and Cormack, U. (1954) 'Casework in Practice', in Morris (1954).

Marshall, T. H. and Leubuscher, C. (1946) *Training for Social Work*, Oxford University Press, Oxford.

Martin, A. E. (1944) 'Child Neglect: A Problem of Social Administration', *Public Administration*, vol. 22(2).

Marx, K. (1974) *Capital: Volume 1*, Lawrence & Wishart, London.

Matza, D. (1969) *Becoming Deviant*, Prentice-Hall, Englewood Cliffs, N.J.

Mayer, J. and Timms, N. (1970) *The Client Speaks*, Routledge & Kegan Paul, London.

Mays, J. B. (1967) *Crime and the Social Structure*, Faber, London.

Means, R. (1977) *Social Work and the Undeserving Poor*, Occasional Paper No. 37, Centre for Urban and Regional Studies, University of Birmingham.

Miliband, R. (1980) 'Class War Conservatism', *New Society*, 19 June.

Mills, C. Wright (1943) 'Professional Ideology of Social Pathologists', *American Journal of Sociology*, vol. 49(2).

Minns, R. (1972) 'Homeless Families and some Organisational Determinants of Deviancy', *Policy and Politics*, vol. 1(1).

Morris, C. (ed.) (1954) *Social Casework in Great Britain*, Faber, London.

Morris, Sir Charles (1964) 'The Future of the Social Services', *Almoner*, vol. 17(3).

Munday, B. (1972) 'What is Happening to Social Work Students?', *Social Work Today*, 15 June.

Navarro, V. (1982) 'The Crisis of the International Capitalist Order and its Implications for the Welfare State', *Critical Social Policy*, vol. 2(1).

Newcastle upon Tyne Trades Council, Centre for the Unemployed (1980) *On the Stones*, Newcastle Trades Council, Newcastle.

Nokes, P. (1967) *The Professional Task in Welfare Practice*, Routledge & Kegan Paul, London.

Novak, T. (1978) 'Poverty and the State', unpublished Ph.D. thesis, University of Durham.

Novak, T. (1980) 'The Social Security Bills', *Bulletin on Social Policy*, no. 5.

Novak, T. (1981) *The Cost of a Plain Coffin: The Tories and Social Security*, Bulletin on Social Policy, Rochdale.

Oakshott, J. E. (1894) *The Humanizing of the Poor Law*, Fabian Tract No. 54.

Oppenheimer, M. (1975) 'The Unionisation of the Professional', *Social Policy*, vol. 5(5).

Parry, N., Rustin, M. and Satyamurti, C. (eds) (1979) *Social Work, Welfare and the State*, Arnold, London.

Parsloe, P., Hill, M. and Stevenson, O. (1978) *Social Work Research Project: Final Report in Three Volumes*, Universities of Aberdeen, Bristol and Keele.

Parton, N. A. (1975) 'What is Social Work Militancy?', *Community Care* (letters), 22 October.

Patel, I. (1972) 'The Learner in Social Work Education', in *Curriculum Development and Teaching*, International Association of Schools of Social Work, Bombay.

Pearson, G. (1973) 'Social Work as the Privatised Solution of Public Ills', *British Journal of Social Work*, vol. 3(2).

Pearson, G. (1975) *The Deviant Imagination*, Macmillan, London.

Pearson, G. (1975a) 'Making Social Workers', in Bailey and Brake (1975).

Pearson, G. (1978) 'Social Work and Law and Order', *Social Work Today*, 4 April.

Phillipson, C. (1981) 'Militant Pensioners', *Bulletin on Social Policy*, no. 8.

Philp, A. F. (1963) *Family Failure*, Faber, London.

Pinker, R. (1979) 'Slimline Social Work', *New Society*, 13 December.

Political and Economic Planning (1948) *Population Policy in Great Britain*, PEP, London.

Rankin, G. (1970) 'Professional Social Work and the Campaign against Poverty', *Social Work Today*, vol. 1(10).

Rees, S. (1976) 'Defining Moral Worthiness', *Social Work Today*, 24 June.

Rodgers, B. N. and Dixon, J. (1960) *Portrait of Social Work*, Oxford University Press, Oxford.

Rodgers, B. N. and Stevenson, J. (1973) *A New Portrait of Social Work*, Heinemann, London.

Royal Commission on Population (1949) *Report on Population*, Cmnd 7695, HMSO, London.

Salford, City of (1950) *The Neglected Child and the Problem Family*, Conference Report.

Scheff, T. (1968) 'Negotiating Reality: Notes on Power in the Assessment of Responsibility', *Social Problems*, vol. 16(1).

Seabrook, J. (1978) *What Went Wrong?*, Gollancz, London.

Seebohm Report (1968) *Report on the Personal and Allied Social Services*, Cmnd 3703, HMSO, London.

Shairp, L. V. (1910) *Hints for Visitors*, Richard Jackson, Leeds.

Simpkin, M. (1983) *Trapped Within Welfare* (2nd edn), Macmillan, London.

Sinfield, A. (1970) 'Which Way for Social Work?', in P. Townsend *et al.*, *The Fifth Social Service*, Fabian Society, London.

Sinfield, A. (1974) 'Poverty and the Social Services Department', in M. Brown (ed.), *Social Issues and the Social Services*, Charles Knight, London.

Smith, E. D. (1957) 'Education and the Task of Making Social Work Professional', *Social Service Review*, vol. 31, March.

Social Workers Action Group (1979) *Social Services in Leeds*, NALGO Local Authority Branch, Leeds.

Spencer, J. and Crookston, L. (1978) 'The Relationship between Local Authority Social Services Departments and the Supplementary Benefits Organisations', 1st draft report, DHSS, London.

Stedman Jones, G. (1971) *Outcast London*, Clarendon Press, Oxford.

Stephens, T. (1945) *Problem Families*, Pacifist Service Units, Liverpool/ Manchester.

Stevenson, O. (1976) 'Social Work — The Courses and the Local Authorities', unpublished paper to the Association of Social Work Teachers.

Strong Words (1979) *But The World Goes on The Same*, Strong Words, Durham.

Taylor, I. (1981) *Law and Order: Arguments for Socialism*, Macmillan, London.

Taylor, I., Walton, P. and Young, J. (1973) *The New Criminology*, Routledge & Kegan Paul, London.

Taylor, I., Walton, P. and Young, J. (1975) *Critical Criminology*, Routledge & Kegan Paul, London.

Taylor, J. (1972) *From Self-Help to Glamour: The Workingman's Club*

1860–1972, History Workshop Pamphlets No. 7, Ruskin College, Oxford.

Taylor Gooby, P. and Dale, J. (1981) *Social Theory and Social Welfare*, Edward Arnold, London.

Thompson, E. P. (1965) 'Peculiarities of the English', *Socialist Register*, Merlin Press, London.

Thompson, E. P. (1968) *The Making of the English Working Class*, Penguin, Harmondsworth.

Thompson, E. P. (1978) *The Poverty of Theory*, Merlin Press, London.

Tilley, M. (1955) 'Casework with the Anti-Social Client', *British Journal of Psychiatric Social Work*, vol. 2, Spring.

Timms, N. and Philp, A. F. (1957) *The Problem of the Problem Family*, Family Service Units, London.

Timms, N. and Watson, D. (eds) (1976) *Talking about Welfare*, Routledge & Kegan Paul, London.

Titmuss, R. M. (1950) *Problems of Social Policy*, HMSO, London.

Titmuss, R. M. (1957) 'Introduction' in Timms and Philp (1957).

Titmuss, R. M. (1969) *Commitment to Welfare*, Allen & Unwin, London.

Towle, C. (1954) *Learner in Education for the Professions*, University of Chicago Press, Chicago.

Townshend, Mrs (1911) *The Case against the COS*, Fabian Tract No. 158.

Training Committee (COS) (1898) *First Report of the Committee on Training*, COS Occasional Paper No. 11.

Unemployment Unit (1981) *A Dossier of Despair*, Unemployment Unit, London.

Urwick, E. J. (1903) 'Social Education of Yesterday and Today', *Charity Organisation Review*, vol. 14.

Urwick, E. J. (1904) 'A School of Sociology', in Loch (1904).

Waldron, F. E. (1958) 'The Angry Client', *Almoner*, vol. 11(2).

Walker, H. and Beaumont, B. (1981) *Probation Work: Critical Theory and Socialist Practice*, Blackwell, Oxford.

Walton, R. G. (1975) *Women in Social Work*, Routledge & Kegan Paul, London.

Weber, M. (1948) *Essays in Sociology*, ed. C. Wright Mills and H. Gerth, Routledge & Kegan Paul, London.

Whetham, W. C. D. (1909) *The Family and the Nation*, Longman & Green, London.

Wilson, D. (1974) 'Uneasy Bedfellows', *Social Work Today*, vol. 5(1).

Wilson, E. (1977) *Women and the Welfare State*, Tavistock, London.

Wilson, E. (1980) *Only Halfway to Paradise*, Tavistock, London.

Wilson, H. C. (1966) 'Pre-School Training of Culturally Deprived Children', *Howard Journal*, vol. 12(1).

Wilson, R. (1949) 'Aims and Methods of a Department of Social Studies', *Social Work* (UK), vol. 6.

Wilson, R. (1950) 'Social Work in a Changing World', *Social Work* (UK), vol. 7, October.

Wolfenden, J. (1959) 'The Family and Moral Standards', *Social Work* (UK), vol. 16(1).

Women's Group on Public Welfare (1943) *Our Towns*, Oxford University Press, Oxford.

Woodard, C. (1961) 'The Charity Organisation Society and the Rise of the Welfare State', unpublished Ph.D. thesis, Cambridge University.

Wootton, B. (1959) *Social Science and Social Pathology*, Allen & Unwin, London.

Wootton, B. (1975) 'A Philosophy for the Social Services', *Socialist Commentary*, January.

Working Party on Marriage Guidance (1979) *Marriage Matters*, HMSO, London.

Wright, R. C. (1977) *Expectations of the Teaching of Social Work in Courses leading to a CQSW*, Consultative Document No. 3, CCETSW, London.

Yeo, C. S. (1973) 'Introduction' to republished edition of Helen Bosanquet's *Social Work in London*, Harvester Press, Brighton.

Younghusband, E. (1947) *Report on the Employment and Training of Social Workers*, Constable, Edinburgh.

Younghusband, E. (1956) 'Trends in Social Work Education', *Social Work*, vol. 13, October.

Younghusband Report (1959) *Report of the Working Party on Social Workers in the Local Authority Health and Welfare Services*, HMSO, London.

Younghusband, E. (1970) 'Social Work and Social Values', *Social Work Today*, vol. 1(4).

Index